BEYOND OUR KEN

A GUIDE TO THE BATTLE FOR LONDON

Andrew Forrester

Stewart Lansley

Robin Pauley

D1513945

FOURTH ESTATE · LONDON

First published in Great Britain in 1985
by Fourth Estate Ltd
100 Westbourne Grove
London W2 5RU

Copyright © 1985 by Robin Pauley and London Weekend Television

Produced by Charmian Allwright

British Library Cataloguing in Publication Data
Forrester, Andrew
    Beyond Our Ken: a guide to the battle for London
    1. Greater London Council
    2. London (England) — politics and government
    II. Pauley, Robin
    III. Lansley, Stewart
    352.0421   JF3631

ISBN 0 947795 90 1

Typeset by Northumberland Press Ltd,
Gateshead, Tyne and Wear
Printed and bound by Richard Clay (The Chaucer Press) Ltd,
Bungay, Suffolk

CONTENTS

Preface and Acknowledgements

This book takes its theme from London Weekend Television's 'London Programme' Special – 'The Battle for London' – on the government's plans for the abolition of the GLC, transmitted on 19 October 1984. Although the book is not directly related to the programme, it covers the same issue and draws on the same themes. Two of the authors are part of the team who produced the programme. The third is Home Affairs correspondent of the *Financial Times*.

In writing the book – which was entirely a joint effort – we wish to thank the following: Dennis Barkway, David Bayliss, Peter Bowness, Bill Bush, John Carvel, Nita Clarke, Bernard Crofton, Lady Denington, Henry Drucker, Norman Flynn, Alan Greengross, Nicholas Hinton, Andy Harris, George Jones, Peter Kellner, Steve Leach, Ken Livingstone, Tony McBrearty, Andrew (Lord) McIntosh, Alan Norton, Anne Sofer, John Stewart, Tony Travers, Carole Vielba, John Wheeler MP, Ken Young; Rod Allen, Jeremy Bugler, David Cox, Lynn Ferguson and Mick Pilsworth of LWT; Tony Oldfield of LWT for graphic design; Dial-A-Ride; the GLC press office; the Local Government Campaign Unit; the Department of the Environment; the staff of the *Financial Times* and LWT libraries; and all those central and local government officials whose 'contributions' have been so helpful, but whose own interests would not be helped by us if we named them.

Our special thanks go to Sarah Mahaffy, without whose efforts this book would never have emerged. We have also relied heavily on a number of written sources which have been listed in the bibliography. Finally we are especially grateful to Rita Barton, Debbie Hall, Jo Mitchell, Anne Syniuk, Pat Turnbull and Cheryl Ward who cheerfully, accurately and with great speed converted our scripts into a final manuscript.

Naturally, all responsibility for the text lies with the authors.

Andrew Forrester, Stewart Lansley, Robin Pauley, Jan. 1985

1. INTO BATTLE

The GLC is typical of this new divisive form of socialism ... so we shall abolish the GLC!
(Norman Tebbit, March 1984)

When Margaret Thatcher met the press to launch the Tory manifesto for the 1983 general election, she pulled one surprise rabbit out of the hat – a pledge to abolish the Greater London Council along with the six metropolitan county councils. Her plan was to transfer their functions to the local boroughs and districts, leaving these major conurbations without an area-wide elected council. Abolition fitted neatly into Mrs Thatcher's overall philosophy. She saw it as streamlining local government by eliminating 'a wasteful and unnecessary tier of government'. In the case of the GLC it also provided what appeared to be a neat way of dealing with Ken Livingstone, the GLC leader, who had become a source of growing irritation to her.

At the time she no doubt also saw the move as being both popular and easy to implement. To her and many others, the GLC, in particular, seemed little more than a bloated bureaucracy fulfilling only a limited range of functions that could, for the most part, be better carried out by the boroughs. It was also a major public joke. Ken Livingstone was almost daily smeared in the popular press, and at the time of the general election was a source of considerable embarrassment to the Labour leadership.

In the event, Mrs Thatcher's renowned instincts have proved badly unreliable. The government has not taken on a simple formality but a gargantuan task, in which the political stakes have become increasingly high. The process of abolition has been dogged by severe political and technical difficulties, and by serious errors of judgement leading to one headache after another.

In the process, it has become increasingly clear that no advance planning had gone into the decision to go for execution. The commitment was made without any evaluation of the ways and means of implementing the decision. Indeed, the proposal had already been considered and rejected by the Cabinet in the eighteen months before May 1983. This absence of forethought has been further compounded by the shrewd – and expensive – defence campaign launched by the GLC itself.

Gradually, opinion has turned against the government, giving rise to mounting opposition from all sides – from the public, the experts and, much more importantly, from within the

Conservative Party itself. Severe doubts have been raised about the validity of the government's claims that abolition would simplify and improve local government, especially in London. Concern has also grown about leaving London as the only capital in Western Europe without an elected council of its own.

In the summer of 1984, as pressure grew against the government's plans, the House of Lords inflicted a decisive – and unexpected – defeat on the first stage of the abolition proposals, leading to an embarrassing change in tactics. Worse still for Mrs Thatcher, Ken Livingstone, far from being bloodlessly eliminated, has been transformed from bogeyman to near popular hero. It is above all Mr Livingstone's campaign against Mrs Thatcher's ill-conceived abolition plans which have projected him into a formidable national figure and political foe.

Despite these hurdles, Mrs Thatcher has shown no sign of flinching in her determination to have her way. The developing battle has provided a classic example of her reputation for firm resolution. In November 1984 the Bill to execute the councils was published and began a long and stormy path through parliament. The government's aim was to have the Bill on the Statute Book by November 1985, in order to abolish the GLC and the other councils in April 1986 – some three years after the election pledge.

Despite the difficulties to date, few pundits really believed that the government would fail to impose its will on parliament. The government, after all, had a formidable majority of 142 in the Commons, and the Lords had rarely moved against legislation enacting manifesto commitments. On the opening day of the committee stages in the House of Commons on 12 December, however, the government suffered a serious backbench revolt at 12.37 a.m. the following morning – 19 Conservatives voted against the government on an amendment to replace the GLC with an elected body whose powers would be decided after a Commons Committee investigation. With many Tories also abstaining, the government's majority slumped to 23.

That rebellion led to renewed speculation about the future of the government's plans and renewed optimism among the abolition opponents that parliament would again force the Cabinet into fundamental changes in its plans. Few predicted that the GLC would actually survive. But substantial amendments aimed at creating some kind of replacement elected body could no longer be ruled out. If this happened, it would be a humiliating setback for Mrs Thatcher. She had already made her own position clear on such a proposal, dubbing it the 'son of Frankenstein'.

Even if the proposals go through, and the GLC disappears in 1986, most observers predict that pressure will mount for the reinstatement of some kind of elected authority. The history of London government will not easily be laid to rest there. The battle for London is likely to be a continuing saga.

The story of that battle is the subject of this book, which concentrates on the current debate but also puts it in historical context. The battle for London hardly began in May 1983. If Mrs Thatcher gets her way she will be putting the clock back 96 years. It was in 1889 that the first elected London-wide council – the London County Council – was established.

That and the subsequent changes in London government have been sharply contested, and are discussed in Chapter 2. This shows that the current struggle over London government is hardly new. Indeed, there are striking historical parallels.

Chapters 3 and 4 put the current debate in its political context. Chapter 3 discusses the importance of Ken Livingstone's attempt to transform the GLC from a largely anonymous, dull and routine body to one with a high and radical public profile presenting a symbolic alternative to the ideology of Mrs Thatcher. Chapter 4 looks at the significance of this personalized conflict in explaining Mrs Thatcher's decision to execute the GLC. How far was the government's decision a simple continuation of the tide of history, how much a genuine concern with improving the efficiency and accountability of local government, and how much a personal vendetta? The chapter reveals the longer-term influences on Mrs Thatcher, including the pressure over many years from London Tory MPs and her antipathy towards the ILEA, as well as the impromptu act the decision has been widely interpreted to be.

Chapter 5 looks at the political fiasco over the government's decision to abolish the GLC elections scheduled for May 1985. Chapter 6 examines the performance of the GLC since it was formed, while Chapter 7 examines the government's proposals for change in detail. While the book concentrates on the GLC itself, Chapter 8 also looks at the position of the metropolitan county councils. Chapter 9 looks at the alternative options for the government of London, revealing a series of possibilities all ignored in the government's proposals. Each of these is likely to be given much more serious consideration if the government's own proposals fall. Chapter 10 is forward-looking. It examines the continuing political and technical hurdles facing the government's proposal, the problems raised by union and borough non-cooperation, and the likelihood of Mrs Thatcher's decision continuing to haunt her until the next general election and beyond.

2. A CENTURY OF CONFLICT

Your so-called municipality is I believe something like ten or twelve times larger than any other municipality in the country ... we should have seen that we might have obtained a much more efficient machine ... if we had been content to look on London as what it is – not as one great municipality but as an aggregate of municipalities. (Lord Salisbury, Conservative Prime Minister, speaking about the 'megalomania' of the London County Council, November 1897)

The Thatcher proposal to abolish the Greater London Council took almost everyone by surprise. But a defiant response soon came from the Labour leaders at County Hall. They announced they were going to fight and immediately got down to the task of drawing up the battle plans. A struggle for the hearts and minds of Londoners was on.

It is not the first time that the question of London government has held the centre of the political stage, and it is unlikely to be the last. If a stormy history stretching over more than 150 years shows anything, it is how difficult it has been to find any lasting solution to the problem of government in the capital.

The reasons for this are complex. London has been both a uniquely large and rapidly changing conurbation. It has, in addition, been afflicted by internal division and clashes of interest. Neither of these factors has made it easy to lay solid foundations for any system of local government. However, London has suffered a further handicap in being the capital city and the seat of government. Because control of the capital has seemed important to governments at Westminster, party political calculations have often intruded to an undesirable degree into proposals for improving the way London is governed.

Throughout the whole of the nineteenth century London was undergoing a staggering transformation. As British trade with the rest of the world expanded rapidly, people flooded into the capital to take employment in its burgeoning docks and workshops, its service industries and its offices. The population grew from just under a million in 1800 to over 7 million in 1900. As this population explosion got under way the built-up area spilled out over the fields and open country in what seemed to be an unstoppable tide of bricks and mortar. The pace of expansion took London far ahead of any other city in the world and made it an object of wonder and admiration. (It had, as we shall see, its darker side.) At the same time it presented a peculiar headache for all those concerned with bringing efficient and democratic local government to the capital. Any boundary that might be drawn would be rendered obsolete by the relentless expansion of the conurbation.

There was a second problem in defining what could properly

be called London. In the early part of the century the term 'London' applied, strictly speaking, only to the ancient square mile of 'The City of London'. The new districts spreading out beyond historic London often had clear identities of their own and did not consider themselves to be part of 'London'. Some of these districts had ancient roots, especially the 'City of Westminster' (the seat both of the crown and of parliament) and, south of the Thames, the medieval suburb of Southwark. Others – expanded villages such as Islington, Hackney or Chelsea – harboured equally strongly their separate sense of distinctiveness. Only very slowly, as the separate villages of London became swallowed up in the expanding urban sprawl, did the idea become established that everyone living in the built-up area belonged to one single 'metropolis' and shared some kind of common interest.

Even then there were other interests that still seemed to keep Londoners apart. On the one hand there was a big divide between 'the City' and the rest. The City had an ancient charter that gave it the right to a 'corporation' and a Lord Mayor. Over the centuries it had become a great financial centre which jealously guarded its trading privileges. The last thing the City authorities wanted was an expansion of its boundaries to take in the new London outside. That would have meant both a change in its constitution – making it more democratic – and, inevitably, the siphoning off of some of its wealth to relieve the growing problems of the poorer areas. To prevent this the City consistently fought any proposal for reform where its interests were conceivably likely to be threatened. In 1837 the power of its lobby at Westminster was enough to kill off the first serious attempt to create an elected London-wide council.

Opposition to the idea of one single council for the 'metropolis', however, did not come only from the City. Other well-to-do areas, such as Paddington and St James's, took up equally independent attitudes for largely similar self-interested reasons.

This alliance of the privileged was mainly responsible for the fact that London continued to lag seriously behind the rest of Britain in winning the right to govern its own affairs according to democratic principles.

The metropolis recognized

In the end, though, circumstances forced parliament to recognize that a conurbation the size of London needed effective local government. In 1848 and 1849 a terrible epidemic of cholera swept through the overcrowded poorer parts of the metropolitan area. In the summer of 1849 13,000 people died in the four hottest months. Although the precise cause of the disease was not yet understood, it was generally accepted to be associated with unhealthy living conditions. Any middle-class visitor to the older and less salubrious parts of the metropolis would be immediately struck not just by the overcrowding but by the dreadful problem posed by the lack of proper sanitary provision. Sewage often gathered in open cesspools or drained away slowly in open ditches.

The inadequacy of the London sewers was one factor in the appointment of a Royal Commission on the City in 1852. Two years later its report recommended a massive shake-up of local government in London. It suggested keeping the City but setting up alongside it seven new 'municipalities' carved out of the rest of the new expanded London. However, it argued that these eight bodies, acting independently, could not reasonably tackle a London-wide problem such as the provision of adequate sewerage. This required planning on an all-London scale. So the Commission proposed a new London-wide body to carry out such 'public works in which all had a common interest'. This Metropolitan Board of Works was to have a governing council on which each of the eight municipalities would be represented.

The Royal Commission Report of 1854 provided one possible, reasonably coherent framework for London local government. But the plan was drastically revised when it went through parliament, as a result of lobbying by well-heeled districts who were opposed to change.

Although London had no properly planned structure of local government in 1854, outside the City there was a rudimentary system of councils based on ancient parish boundaries, the so-called vestries. There were no fewer than 170 such bodies in the proposed Metropolitan Board area. They varied enormously in size and effectiveness.

The man who had the job of piloting the Bill through parliament was a London MP, Sir Bernard Hall. His own constituency housed one of the most powerful of the vestries, that based on the parish of St Marylebone. Like many other better-off vestries, St Marylebone was utterly opposed to the Royal Commission scheme. In the face of the political objections coming from the vestries and the City of London, Sir Bernard decided to make drastic modifications to the original plan. When the new Metropolitan Management Act finally emerged in 1855 all trace of the proposed seven new boroughs had disappeared. Instead the City stayed as it was and was jointly represented on the new Board of Works by 23 of the largest vestries and 15 'vestry boards' which each represented groups of the smaller ones.

The 'joint board' outcome of 1855 never looked likely to provide a lasting solution. Yet the arrangement was to endure for over 30 years. This was largely the outcome of a failure, even among those who strongly favoured reform, to agree on the form any new local government should take. Throughout the period argument raged between those who supported what might be termed the 'localist' solution of breaking London up into separate boroughs and those who favoured a 'centralist' approach of having just one big and powerful council for the capital. Increasingly, over the years, the localist position got the support of London's Conservatives and of spokesmen for the wealthier areas. They saw the single-council scheme as a threat to the pockets of the better-off, just as the City had done. Understandably, for the same reason, the centralist solution was advocated by London's radical liberal politicians, who represented the poorer districts which stood to gain most if rates raised in the richer areas could be used to tackle the problem of overcrowding and the festering slums that went with it.

A county council for London

When reform did finally come, in 1889, it was the centralist position that came out on top. By a strange irony the reform was carried through by a Conservative government at Westminster. Why events took this turn can be explained only by the developing parliamentary politics of the period.

In 1883 a Liberal government under Gladstone had tried to introduce a single London council solution based on expanding the City of London outwards to encompass the whole area over which the Metropolitan Board of Works held responsibility. Characteristically, this had met opposition from the City itself. In the end the scheme foundered on a disagreement within the Cabinet over who should control the Metropolitan Police (since its foundation in 1829 the force had answered directly to the Home Secretary. Other police forces were at least nominally subject to local council control). Then in 1886 the Liberal Party was torn asunder by Gladstone's conversion to Irish Home Rule.

Those who opposed Home Rule, the Liberal Unionists, crossed the floor of the House in large enough numbers to ensure Gladstone's downfall, and a new minority Conservative government was formed by Lord Salisbury. Quite coincidentally, most Liberal Unionists were strong supporters of local government reform. Their leader, Joseph Chamberlain, was a Radical who had built his political reputation as the Mayor of Birmingham. Chamberlain was the country's leading exponent of 'municipal' enterprise. Between 1873 and 1876, he was later to boast, Birmingham had been 'parked, paved, assized, marketed, gas-and-watered, and *improved* – all as the result of three years' work'. Chamberlain had only just launched his 'Radical Programme', and one of its key proposals was to extend the benefits of local democracy to England's rural areas. He advocated a system of elected 'county councils' to take over from the centuries-old system of administration by Justices of the Peace.

To secure the new Conservative–Liberal Unionist alliance Salisbury agreed that his government would introduce such a scheme. A year later, in 1887, the County Councils Bill was introduced into parliament. In the event it contained a political bombshell: it proposed creating a new 'County' of London, with the same boundaries as, and to take the place of, the old Metropolitan Board of Works. The most remarkable aspect of the plan – introduced, after all, by a Conservative government – was its failure to make any gesture towards the localist cause that London's Conservatives had, up to then, so enthusiastically embraced. The scheme provided for no 'second tier' of local authorities that could give some expression to the local pride

GLC Photo Library

First Meeting of the London County Council, 1889.

and local interests of such places as Westminster or Kensington.

The apparent volte-face on the part of the Conservatives had come about largely by accident. The scheme for a new County of London was the brainchild of the East London Tory MP who had been put in charge of the legislation, Charles Ritchie. His original idea had been to slot in a new layer of 'district councils' beneath the proposed LCC to satisfy the supporters of localism. But in the end he was persuaded to drop these provisions for reasons of short-term expediency: it was agreed that they made the Bill so long and complicated that they would threaten its safe passage through parliament. The effect of this was to make the new London County Council even more powerful than had been anticipated.

Even so it is worth noting that, from the outset, the LCC suffered from a fairly obvious flaw. Its boundaries were set for the Board of Works in 1855. By 1889 the population had almost doubled and had spilled over into the surrounding counties. What was meant by 'London', therefore, still defied administrative definition.

The new local authority, however, got off to a good start. In its first elections there was a turnout of 50 per cent, high by present-day standards, and public interest continued to be strong throughout the 1890s. For the 4 million people who lived within its boundaries it helped build up a sense of being 'Londoners'. They looked to the Council for the provision of a wide range of services, including such mundane things as the cleaning and lighting of streets as well as such vital public utilities as a London Fire Service and the provision of sewerage and drainage. Quite rapidly the LCC was to add to its empire two more highly important services. In the 1890s it began to move into the field of public housing and to tackle the enormous task of slum clearance. In 1904 it assumed responsibility for the education service and became overnight the largest local education authority in the world.

All the same it soon became clear that, while the Act of 1889 solved some of the problems of governing London, it created another that has remained ever since. Any really large council like the LCC, with a population greater than many sovereign states, was bound to offer itself as a political power base. In a capital city this was sure to create a potential source of conflict with central government. By 1897 the Conservatives at Westminster, still led by Lord Salisbury, were rather in the position of Doctor Frankenstein, horrified by the creature they had created.

Almost from the moment of its birth the LCC was a troublesome child. In the first elections of 1889 a large majority of the seats were won by the so-called Progressive Party, a grouping of radical liberals, representatives of labour and the odd socialist. The Progressives were keen advocates of using the wealth of London to tackle the problems of the urban poor. To this end they launched an immediate attack on the City of London, deliberately omitted by Charles Ritchie from the LCC. The Conservatives rallied to the defence of the City's interests.

The struggle over the future of the City was to last for many years. At one point (when the Liberals held precarious control at Westminster) the LCC actually secured a Royal Commission to work out the details of the takeover. The City faced a real threat of extinction. This was one reason for Lord Salisbury to take action when he returned to Downing Street in 1895.

But a more important challenge to government came over

the whole question of who was to control the Metropolitan Police. The Progressives saw no good reason why the capital's policemen should not be the responsibility of the LCC, and campaigned vigorously for an end to their control by the Home Office. It is hard to appreciate now how much a threat this seemed to Conservative MPs at the time. Memories of the Paris Commune of 1870–1 still lingered on, and the Tories were haunted by the nightmare of a politically controlled police force standing aside as the 'mob' stormed parliament.

In 1897 Lord Salisbury, who had supported the idea of a large council for London only eight years previously, dramatically announced that he had had a change of heart. He had swung back sharply towards the traditional Conservative view of London. Speaking to London Conservatives, he admitted to past mistakes. The LCC was clearly too large an organization and it would have been better to see London not as 'one great municipality, but as an aggregate of municipalities'.

Lord Salisbury's compromise

Lord Salisbury's plan was a much weaker LCC which would have to play second fiddle to a new set of local boroughs. That way, he announced, the 'megalomania' of the LCC would be effectively curbed. But the outcome was to be a sharp lesson to Westminster politicians that reforming government in the capital was no easy matter. Lord Salisbury committed himself to his plan without consulting his Cabinet colleagues. Many of them took a far less strong line. They feared that the LCC had already established itself as a popular organization with many Londoners and that a frontal attack by a Conservative government on a Progressive-controlled LCC would only hand a great propaganda weapon to the opposition.

So it was to prove. In the LCC elections of 1898 the Progressives fought on a platform to save the LCC. The government's plans, they claimed, would create a squabbling, disunited London, too weak to stand up for the interests of Londoners. The outcome was that the 'Moderates' – as the Conservative supporters on the LCC were then called – lost 11 seats and the Progressives gained 12. It was, in the words of *The Times*, 'a crushing defeat' for the Conservative cause.

Lord Salisbury had committed his government to legislation, but he now radically altered his plans. The scheme for powerful London boroughs was scrapped; instead the new boroughs were to have very little power indeed. The final outcome was the London Government Act of 1899 which set up a new lower tier of 28 'metropolitan boroughs'. The Act gave each borough the right to a mayor, some other trappings that went with borough status, and very little else. Lord Salisbury's opponents could mock the new Act as a 'legislative mouse'. He felt that the groundwork had been laid for a more effective localist solution in the future.

The pattern for local government for London set in 1899 was to last for 65 years, a period that saw some further consolidation of LCC power. This is not to say that dissatisfaction with the arrangements was not expressed forcefully from time to time. Even in the 1900s new suburbs continued to grow up outside the LCC boundary, and at the same time the LCC area began to suffer a decline in population. As early as 1903 H. G. Wells, a leading socialist as well as a writer of science fiction, projected the need for one 'mammoth municipality' to cover the whole London region. The people who lived in the new suburbs largely made their living by 'commuting' into London on the new underground railways, by tramcar or by omnibus. They should be seen as part of 'Greater London' and be planned for and serviced by a single local council.

Wells's ideas were influential, especially among a growing body of socialists. But his scheme failed to give sufficient weight to how the new suburbanites viewed London. Many of those moving out to live in suburbs like Barnet, Wimbledon or Bromley saw themselves as 'escaping' from London to live in semi-rural bliss. The political obstacles in the way of creating a council for Greater London were bound to be formidable. After the First World War a Royal Commission (under Viscount Ullswater) was set up to consider the question and came out in favour of keeping things as they were, largely because of the strength of opposition to any enlarging of the LCC it found in the outer districts.

The report of the Ullswater Commission in 1922 effectively removed the government of the capital from the national political agenda for more than a decade, even if the continuing decline of LCC population and expansion of the suburbs left the issue ticking away like a time bomb that would eventually have to go off. In the end, it was a change in the party balance at County Hall – since 1922 the prestigious custom-built head-quarters of the LCC – that restored the government of the capital to the centre of the political stage.

From 1907 to 1934 the LCC was more or less under constant 'Municipal Reformer' (or Conservative) control. But in the elections of 1934 a new political party and a new political leader took over at County Hall. The Labour Party, throughout the 1920s, had steadily replaced the Progressives as the party of the left. Now, at last, they won a majority of LCC seats and were able to force the Tories out of office.

The LCC under Herbert Morrison

Herbert Morrison, who became leader of the LCC in 1934, had already established himself as a national politician, serving as Minister of Transport in the minority Labour government of 1929–31. Indeed, had it not been for his defeat in the 1931 general election when he lost his seat in Woolwich East, he could well have become leader of the Labour Party in preference to Clement Attlee. Instead, he had turned his hand to securing London for Labour.

The Labour campaign of 1934 was fought on the issue that the Municipal Reformers had been in power too long. After 27 years of their rule it was time for a change. Labour promised to speed up the housing programme and generally to improve services. Their strategy worked and, with the help of a collapse in the Liberal vote, Herbert Morrison and his team were swept into power at County Hall.

The period of Herbert Morrison's leadership took London up to the outbreak of war. It was to show how effective a local authority the LCC could be and, partly as a result, to reopen the thorny question of relations between a powerful LCC and central government.

In terms of powers and responsibilities, the LCC had now reached its zenith. It provided for public housing (in the 1920s opening many out-country estates in the surrounding counties), public education and recreation on a massive scale. It provided the fire and ambulance services for the capital. It was the planning authority and was responsible for London's main roads. Only recently central government had handed over to it the duty of caring for the destitute and the mentally ill, expanding its existing role as a health authority providing clinics and hospitals for Londoners.

If the LCC had become a giant, Herbert Morrison regarded it as sleeping or, at best, half-awake. During a period of economic restraint he was determined to improve the LCC services without throwing enormous burdens on to the ratepayers.

His achievements were impressive. When he took office the Municipal Reformers' housing programme had almost come to a stop as a result of cuts in government housing subsidies. The new Labour administration at County Hall was pledged to tackle the still pressing problems presented by slum housing – quickly. So one of its first acts was to embark on a vast programme of building that laid new stress on flats rather than houses. By 1937 Herbert Morrison could claim that, in a single year, the LCC had demolished over 2,000 buildings and provided homes for over 20,000 people. An enthusiastic film documentary of the period drove the message home as it depicted shabby but happy working-class families moving out of their old slum properties into sparkling new art-deco flats.

Morrison was even more proud of what the LCC achieved in modernizing its hospitals and installing the very latest medical technology. This even extended to wireless sets for patients. With a similar human touch, holidays at the seaside were introduced for the patients in the LCC long-stay mental hospitals. In a very real sense – in the words of his biographer, Professor George Jones – Herbert Morrison was creating 'a mini-welfare state': it was a 'try-out' for the future Labour government of 1945. His LCC improved other services (in education, for instance, it dabbled with 'modern' methods), but all this was achieved with only a small increase in the rates bill. This reflected the power a large organization like the LCC had

GLC Photo Library

Herbert Morrison at County Hall. He put the LCC on the map like never before.

in being able to borrow money at very competitive rates of interest.

The verdict of the electorate was to be enthusiastic. In the 1937 LCC elections more electors turned out (up from only 33 per cent in 1934 to 43 per cent) and Labour was confirmed in power with an increased majority. This was all, of course, of interest to the reigning Conservative government at Westminster. Herbert Morrison had become one of the best-known politicians not just in London, but across the country and he was soon to show he was even capable of inflicting humiliating defeat on government ministers.

This happened in the case of the demolition of the old

Waterloo Bridge. The bridge had been designed by Rennie and had a certain architectural distinction, but by the 1920s it was clearly inadequate for the traffic it had to carry and had begun to crumble. When Herbert Morrison came to power at County Hall in 1934 there had been talk for years of demolishing it and putting up a new structure, but now the government had suddenly changed tack. It had come up with a new scheme to preserve and widen the old bridge which had not impressed Herbert Morrison at all. He reckoned that even a widened bridge would be inadequate. However, the government was adamant that it could not now provide a grant to pay for any new bridge. Other LCC leaders might have left it at that, but not Herbert Morrison. He argued that the LCC was rich enough simply to go ahead with the project and pay for it directly out of the rates. Within a few weeks he personally conducted the symbolic act of casting down the first stone of the old bridge. Three years later – as demolition was completed – he rubbed salt into the government's wounds by persuading it that a grant should be provided after all, in order to give the minister some say in the building of the new structure and because the government needed the cooperation of the LCC to deal with the capital's growing traffic problems!

In the meantime Herbert Morrison had led Labour to victory in the LCC elections of 1937, and this was to set the alarm bells ringing in Conservative Central Office. The control of the capital seemed politically important to them and it was becoming more and more clear that Conservative chances of regaining control of the LCC were fast diminishing.

The thirties had witnessed a new explosion of suburbs out into the Home Counties. The expansion of the Underground system and the coming of the motor omnibus and the motorcar had opened up people's horizons. Estate after estate of speculative housing had swept over parts of Middlesex, Essex, Surrey and Kent. In the eight years from 1931 to 1939 the population of the Home Counties rose by over a million while that of the LCC area began to fall more rapidly. Many of the people moving out to suburbia were natural supporters of the Conservatives. They bought their own houses, tended to have white-collar jobs and were upwardly mobile. On the other hand those who continued to live in the area controlled by County Hall were increasingly the poor, the council tenants and those with less well-paid employment, the sort of people who would in general look towards the Labour Party as best representing their interests.

The gloom that had descended on Conservative Party head-quarters in 1938 was based on an analysis of these social trends. Already party officials were suggesting that the only way to break the socialist stranglehold at County Hall was to redraw the boundaries of the LCC. Sooner or later political pressure was bound to be put on Conservative ministers to put the whole question of the government of the capital back into the melting pot.

There were other, less political pressures also building up for a radical reform of the LCC. By 1939 the population of Greater London had risen to eight and a half million but the LCC area contained less than half of this total. This made the LCC look out of date as a council for the capital. More importantly, developments in transport and the influx of new industries enormously increased the case for planning the whole conurbation. Many of the new suburbs had grown up in an unplanned way without any consideration of their impact on London as a whole. Yet their growth had obvious implications for central London, especially in terms of traffic congestion and roads policy. In the 1930s the LCC did what it could by developing a 'green belt' policy to try to stop the open country-side around the capital being entirely swallowed up. But it could do this only by paying surrounding local authorities to cooperate with the scheme. Increasingly, in the late 1930s, more and more voices were calling for one overall planning authority for the whole metropolitan region. As the LCC celebrated its jubilee in 1939 a famous critique of London government was published by William Robson, a rising star at the London School of Economics. *The Government and Misgovernment of London* highlighted the 'present makeshift muddle' and pro-posed the creation of a vast new London-wide local authority. In the event, only the outbreak of war put a brake on this academic and political offensive to abolish the LCC.

The coming of the GLC

It was not until the 1950s that the question was to be reopened. Following the war Labour was in power at Westminster and, with Herbert Morrison* in the Cabinet, was never likely to tinker with what had become its major power base in southern Britain. Rather there was a tendency to place such questions as the planning of London in the hands of Whitehall civil servants.

On the other hand the Conservatives, who began their 13-year control of parliament in 1951, had always distrusted the view that 'Whitehall knows best' and had a clear political motive for attacking the LCC. Even so it was not until 1957 that the first major step was taken down the road that was to lead to the destruction of that by now venerable body. Pressures to take action came both from within the civil service and from the ranks of the Conservative Party, but they had different and contradictory objectives. The outcome was to be a highly unsatisfactory compromise that would keep the question of London government open right down to the present day.

The civil servants at the then Ministry of Housing and Local Government basically sought to 'tidy up' local government in the capital in order to make it more logical, more efficient and, at the same time, capable of taking on the massive task of planning for London. The views of these civil servants impressed the Royal Commission set up in 1957 under Sir Edwin Herbert to consider the matter.

Conservatives in the London area were, on the other hand, much more interested in breaking up the LCC in the old localist tradition. Those who represented the outer London areas were the more powerful within the party. As suburbanites they did not generally consider themselves to be 'Londoners' at all. In their view any new local government structure would have to recognize the near autonomy of each constituent part of so-called 'Greater London'.

* It is interesting that, as a young politician, Herbert Morrison had favoured reorganizing London along Robson lines. He changed his view after his experience of what could be achieved by the LCC and never wavered in his support for its retention.

The Herbert Commission tried to reconcile these conflicting points of view. Its report, published in 1960, advocated a two-tier system of government. The lower tier, or 'London boroughs', were to be more important than the old 'metropolitan boroughs' of 1899. They were to run all the personal services such as housing, children's homes and home helps. They were to administer a local education service. In planning they were to be given limited powers to deal with planning applications. In the words of the Herbert Commission they were to be the 'primary units' of local government, running as much as was practically possible from the local town hall or civic centre.

However, the Royal Commission accepted the case for a 'council for Greater London' – to take charge of matters too broad for the local borough to handle. This all-London council would prepare a development plan for the whole metropolitan area which was defined as extending, broadly speaking, to the limits of the built-up area. It would deal with the anticipated continual pressure of population in Greater London – largely by making 'overspill' arrangements with local authorities elsewhere – and it would plan for London's anticipated new roads and for the location of new industry, offices and housing development. It would also plan for and control the resources of the education service run by the proposed London boroughs.

The commissioners saw these planning functions as being extremely important and clearly saw their proposals as making for a real devolution of decision-making from Whitehall. The new top-tier authority would, in effect, restore to Londoners some democratic control over the everyday world that surrounded them.

Some critics of the Herbert Report, including the now Professor William Robson, felt its proposals gave too much power to the London boroughs, especially in the field of planning. But after its publication the political pressures on the government all tended to push it towards a further weakening of the proposed all-London council. This pressure came from the largely Conservative suburban fringe. In its own reaction to the Herbert Commission's proposals the government felt it had to make a gesture to the anti-London sentiment which ran so strongly in places like Bromley and Epsom. It promised that

LONDON COUNTY COUNCIL:
GREATER LONDON COUNCIL
THEIR POWERS COMPARED

KEY:
PLANNING = major authority
Education = power shared with other authorities

LCC	GLC
EDUCATION: *all London schools and colleges in LCC area*	Education: *part-share with London boroughs in inner London only (ILEA)*
HOUSING: *major public housing function in LCC area and outside it*	Housing: *small 'strategic' housing function. Ex LCC/GLC estates to be transferred to boroughs*
PLANNING: *main authority*	Planning: *shared with boroughs*
Transport: *tram cars only*	TRANSPORT: *London Transport (1969–1984)*
ROADS: *main road authority*	ROADS: *Metropolitan roads (largely Ex LCC)*
TRAFFIC: *traffic authority for Inner London (LCC)*	TRAFFIC: *traffic authority for whole GLC area*
REFUSE: *disposal only*	REFUSE: *disposal only*
DRAINAGE AND SEWERAGE	Drainage and sewerage: *transferred to Thames Water Authority (1974)*
FIRE AND CIVIL DEFENCE Cultural Activities: *Arts (especially South Bank), Museums, Historic Buildings*	FIRE AND CIVIL DEFENCE Cultural Activities: *Arts (especially South Bank), Museums, Historic Buildings*

RECREATION: *all major parks*	Recreation: *some parks*
HEALTH AND WELFARE: Major responsibilities: *Hospitals (to 1948), Mental* *Health, Health Centres,* *Domiciliary Services, Children in* *Care, Ambulance Service, Grants*	Health and Welfare: *Grants, Ambulance service* *(to 1974)*

each of these outer areas would be able to 'make known its views about its inclusion in or exclusion from the London area'.

This gave the committed 'localist' politicians of outer London a strong negotiating counter in the subsequent talks. The outcome was that the London Government Act of 1963 significantly increased the powers of the boroughs at the expense of the new Greater London Council. The outer boroughs, for instance, took full charge of normal school education; the anticipated GLC role was dropped. Inner London schools (those run by the old LCC education service) were grouped under an Inner London Education Authority. The ILEA was to be run from County Hall, but under a controlling body consisting of GLC and Inner London Borough councillors, with its own budgeting and rating powers. More importantly the boroughs became planning authorities, contrary to the Herbert recommendations. It was the borough, not the GLC, that would have responsibility for its own district plans. The GLC was reduced to relying on the boroughs, in effect, for the implementation of its own Greater London Plan.

When the new Greater London Council first met in 1964 at County Hall it may have seemed to have donned the mantle of the old LCC. In fact it was a much weaker authority with far fewer powers. The new members gathered, uncertain of the job they had to do and unsure of how to go about it. There was, too, one surprising feature of the first GLC. It had a Labour majority. So many strong Tory areas like Epsom and Esher had won their right to 'keep out' of London that the natural Conservative majority had been destroyed.

The new GLC seemed to set a pattern for the future. It was to concentrate on 'strategic' metropolitan issues, especially strategic planning, while the boroughs were left to run most of the council services. Some services, like the Fire Brigade and the disposal of both sewage and household refuse, were considered to require an all-London approach and were therefore left in the hands of County Hall.

In 1968 another Royal Commission on Local Government was set up to look at arrangements for a new local government structure elsewhere in England, and was clearly influenced by the experience of London. When the Redcliffe-Maud Commission reported in 1969 it suggested three similar 'metropolitan' authorities for England's other large conurbations. Ultimately this led to the creation of the 'metropolitan county councils' in 1974. However, by that time the economic climate of the sixties, which provided much of the logic for big strategic authorities, had begun to change. To the Herbert Commission the biggest challenge facing the new council for Greater London was to be the management of economic growth: the council had to plan for 'overspill' from London and for the better distribution of jobs and community services within the capital. This was to be done through the preparation and implementation of the Greater London Development Plan.

Now, in the seventies, the downturn in the economy was making that sort of planning increasingly irrelevant. The GLC began to find its very existence being questioned, not least by the increasingly confident London borough leaders. The GLC was not in a strong position to fight back. It had never won a place in the heart of Londoners, as the old London County Council had apparently done. This was partly because it controlled far fewer services and was perceived as less important. But it suffered, too, from a see-sawing of political control. Whereas the LCC had remained under Labour control for 30 years (and before that under Conservative control for more than 20 years), the new GLC was balanced on a political knife-edge from the start. There have so far been six GLC elections, and on only one occasion did the party in power at County Hall manage to retain control. This produced a lack of continuity in policy which council officials (many of whom had come from the LCC) found great difficulty in coping with. This was particularly so when Labour and Conservative policies differed so radically. For instance, under the Tories in the late 1960s the planners were encouraged to think in terms of building a network of urban motorways. When Labour won in 1973 the entire motorway programme was abandoned. Again, Labour wanted to build up the GLC strategic housing role; the Tories wanted to see it very much diminished. This switching back and forward on policy made it very difficult for any GLC initiative to be carried through to fruition.

Possibly reflecting this lack of achievement, Londoners seemed to put national issues first when they voted in GLC elections, so that control of County Hall was usually a reflection of who was in power in Westminster. Labour won in 1973 when the Tories under Edward Heath were proving unpopular. The Conservatives won back control in 1977 when the Callaghan government was going through its mid-term crisis. It was no surprise when Labour came back to power in 1981 after two years of the first Thatcher government.

Few GLC politicians made any real impact on the London public in the way Herbert Morrison and other LCC leaders had done. The Tories provided one exception when the colourful Horace Cutler took over in 1977. It increasingly looked as though only someone like Mr Cutler, with a touch of show-business personality, could actually get through to an apathetic public.

In 1981 a hitherto little-known politician called Ken Livingstone became leader of the new Labour-controlled GLC. He was to show what could be done.

3. KEN LIVINGSTONE'S LONDON

You see ... I ... I have a dream. I see it now ... I see Greater London as a land of milk and honey. A land with a gay adventure playground on every street corner. A land where the Special Patrol Group helps old black lesbian ladies to cross the street. A land of free bus travel for the terminally ill, a land of street festivals for one-parent families, a land of free classes in socialist aerobics, a land of reggae and salsa, a land of touring comedies in the Marxist-Leninist tradition, a land of discos for the disabled, a land of culture, a land where the National Theatre caters to the needs of the ordinary sociologist in the street, a land where any man or woman, whatever his or her colour, creed, race, sexual orientation or tastes in underwear can stand up proudly and say, this is my ...' (Red Strephon, alias Ken Livingstone, in *The Ratepayers' Iolanthe*)

Few national politicians in recent memory, let alone local government politicians, have enjoyed such a spectacular rise as Ken Livingstone. Within the space of two years he has jumped from a third-division local councillor to a politician of national stature, rarely out of the media spotlight. At the age of 39 he has led Europe's largest local authority, has seen his first biography emerge (John Carvel's *Citizen Ken*), has been the central character of a popular opera (*The Ratepayers' Iolanthe*) and of a television sit-com ('Struggle').

In the course of his leadership of the GLC, his relations with the media have performed a startling somersault. In the early days he became the subject of increasingly vitriolic press coverage that reached a peak over his contentious and openly expressed views on Northern Ireland, which at one stage led the *Sun* to describe him as 'the most odious man in Britain'.

Yet Mr Livingstone soon became an instant TV personality. At first people appeared to be tuning in to find out what this red monster from London was really like. What they discovered was a man who, on TV at least, was charming, articulate, witty and always able to outmanoeuvre political opponents without being overbearing, rude or pompous. TV ratings rose if he appeared, he was a TV 'natural' and his easy-going boy-next-door approach was a great success. Within little more than a few months he was to emerge as a widely sought after chat-show guest, appearing on programmes as diverse as 'Question Time' and LWT's 'After Midnight' as a guest presenter. In 1982, he was elected second only to the Pope in BBC Radio's Man of the Year poll. In the *Guardian* (17 June 1984) the features editor, Richard Gott, linked him with Tony Benn as one of

only two figures in the Labour Movement who are natural leaders, men who can encapsulate in words and images the often inarticulate aspirations and hopes of hundreds of thousands of ordinary people.

In November 1984, writing in a new magazine, *Options for Men*, Brian Walden, presenter of LWT's 'Weekend World', included Ken Livingstone as one of his eight heroes of the decade, likely 'to have the Labour movement under his thumb' in ten years' time.

But whether Ken Livingstone is a demon or a prophet, over-

or underrated, and whatever his future fortunes, no one can doubt his significance in the battle over the GLC, least of all Mrs Thatcher.

Ken Livingstone's rise

Ken Livingstone joined the Labour Party in 1968, in the South London constituency of Norwood. He was 23. Like many young enthusiasts at the time, he was quickly press-ganged into key offices in both the local branch and the constituency party. By 1971 he had been elected on to Lambeth Council, became vice-chair of the Housing Committee for two years, and remained on the council until 1978. In 1973 he was elected on to the GLC. In 1978 he left Lambeth and became a Camden council-lor, serving as Chair of Housing for two years. He stood for parliament, unsuccessfully, for Hampstead in the 1979 election.

It was during this period that he was to develop his natural political instincts. He was always a convictional rather than a theoretical politician, and it was his close involvement in the political battles in local government during the 1970s that was to shape his overall outlook. For years the Labour Party in local government had been dominated by the centre and right. The left had shown little interest, concentrating on national and industrial issues. From the mid-1970s, this began to change.

This change owed a good deal to the influence of Ted Knight. Mr Knight was a former full-time organizer for the Trotskyist Socialist Labour League (now the Workers' Revolutionary Party). He had been expelled from the Labour Party in the 1950s and was readmitted in 1970. He too was elected to Lambeth Council in 1971 and soon became Chair of Norwood Labour Party. Under his tutelage, Ken Livingstone soon became embroiled in local Labour left–right battles over council policies.

But these early internal squabbles were nothing compared with what was to come later. In the first 12 months of the new Wilson government elected in 1974, local government spending grew. Then in 1975 and 1976, under growing economic diffi-culties and pressure from the International Monetary Fund, the government reversed this expansion, launching a series of cuts in public spending, especially on local councils.

Ken Livingstone was closely involved in the battles over spending levels which ensued in both Lambeth Council and the GLC. Along with Ted Knight, he was also to spearhead wider campaigns against cuts in public services.

It was from these battles that the left gradually emerged with growing influence within the Labour Party, especially in local government and especially in London. In 1977 the left gained a majority – for the first time – on the Regional Executive of the London Labour Party. In 1978 Ted Knight captured the leadership of Lambeth Council, decisively defeating David Stimpson, the former moderate leader. This was the first London Council to fall to the left. Outside London David Blunkett, another left-winger, became leader of Sheffield Council in 1980.

Along with Ted Knight, Ken Livingstone was a central figure in the growing strength of the left in London local government. He had drive, motivation and ambition. He also had time. In 1971, with the support of his wife, Christine, he chose to become a full-time political activist, giving himself opportunities denied to most of his contemporaries.

An effective orator and, above all, a skilful organizer, he gradually emerged as the natural leader of the left in London. At the same time as he was spearheading anti-cuts campaigns he was building a new network of young radical supporters and activists who were, like himself, increasingly disillusioned with the performance of the Labour government and traditional Labour policies. To strengthen the organization of the left, he and several colleagues launched a new left monthly in February 1980 called *London Labour Briefing*. Slowly but surely, an effective power base had emerged for Ken Livingstone's eventual rise to the leadership of the GLC.

In 1979, in a County Hall debate on the future of the GLC, Mr Livingstone had dismissed it as largely irrelevant. This reflected growing disillusion with its role and effectiveness. Then he changed his mind. He decided to make the GLC his personal target.

First he set out to maximize the influence of the left on the new GLC. From the panel of candidates, he wrote to all those who were on the left 'in the broadest sense', sending a list of constituencies in order of winnability, urging them to seek selection in the winnable seats. This plan was to play a crucial role in his succession to the leadership on the day after the elections in May 1981.

In 1980, Reg Goodwin stood down as leader of the GLC Labour Group and Andrew McIntosh defeated Ken Livingstone by one vote in the election for the new leader. It was Mr McIntosh who therefore led Labour into the 1981 elections. During the campaign, the Tories made much of the left's advance in the London Labour Party and of Mr Livingstone's widely known intention to seek the leadership again after the elections. Partly in consequence, though Labour won the elections, the swing to Labour in London was less than elsewhere.

Just a few hours after the elections, a meeting of the newly elected members replaced Mr McIntosh with Mr Livingstone. This was achieved with the aid of a handful of centrists and right-wingers as well as the large body of left-wingers. Simultaneously, almost all the committee chairs were taken by the left, many of them newcomers.

Ken Livingstone had not just set out to increase the number of left GLC councillors, he also worked to influence the manifesto. In the past, manifestos had usually been hurriedly put together by a small caucus of inner party leaders and officials. Mr Livingstone transformed this by organizing, nearly two years in advance of the elections, a series of policy meetings on such key topics as transport, housing, planning and industrial policy. Initially open to all party members, these led to consultative discussions in each policy area which eventually emerged in the most detailed, most comprehensive and longest Labour GLC manifesto ever.

Since 1981, Ken Livingstone and the GLC have rarely been out of the news headlines – most of them highly critical, often vitriolic. This began with stinging attacks from most of Fleet Street over Mr Livingstone's defeat of the moderate Mr McIntosh. Suddenly Ken Livingstone had been elevated from a minor local politician into a public figure. He was newsworthy. Almost immediately some popular newspapers despatched reporters to watch him, to burrow in his dustbins, and to talk to and harass his colleagues and enemies. Their task was to uncover the dirt on Ken Livingstone. To their chagrin, none was found. He had a clean past. Although he had by now split up with his wife, there were no scandals.

From then on, however, Ken Livingstone was to provide the media with no shortage of material. He loved the limelight. He had gained every politician's dream, publicity. In the early days of his leadership, much of this publicity surrounded his incursions into 'foreign policy'. Mr Livingstone did not only set about changing the role of the GLC, he also used his new position to promote his views on wider issues, such as royalty and sexual politics, but especially on Northern Ireland, including support for the IRA hunger-strikers, for discussions with Sinn Fein leader, Gerry Adams, and for immediate withdrawal of British troops. It was this that the media latched on to, with coverage of his controversial outlook becoming increasingly hostile.

As a result of his diversions, fuelled by the sometimes hysterical press responses, Ken Livingstone became increasingly unpopular. Rarely a week went by without some new controversy over him. Although much of the press coverage was exaggerated, and sometimes contrived, he himself was hardly an innocent victim. He rarely went out of his way to avoid publicity, or to exercise caution in his views or the way he presented them. He also had a propensity for indiscreet remarks, which were inevitably quickly pounced on by the press. During the height of this publicity, around the summer and autumn of 1981, he became the subject of widespread criticism within the GLC Labour Group, including the left, for diverting attention away from council policies on to himself. At one stage it was touch and go whether he would survive as leader.

But survive he did. And gradually his image began to change. Moreover, although his early notoriety was closely related to forages into national and international issues, the policies of the GLC quickly became newsworthy. They also brought the council into inevitable conflict with the government. And it was this conflict in turn which must have added to Mrs Thatcher's determination to rid herself of Ken Livingstone and his GLC.

The battle over spending

The first source of conflict with Westminster involved the GLC's overall level of spending. When Labour regained control in May 1981, they were committed to a substantial increase in spending on transport subsidies, job creation schemes and a rents freeze. This contrasted sharply with the government's policy of lower local government spending. It coincided too with the government's new and tighter penalties for overspending. A clash was inevitable. And it came over fares.

The central plank of Labour's programme was a carefully planned and costed cut in bus and tube fares of 25 per cent. Their manifesto had openly warned that the cost − estimated at £100m − would be met by a supplementary rate of 5p in the £. This estimate, however, had not allowed for Michael Heseltine's more punitive system of grant penalties introduced in April 1981, which, unknown when the manifesto was drawn up, doubled the cost to ratepayers of the fares cut.

Far from backing off, however, the GLC stuck to its guns, with support from all sections of the Labour Group, including Andrew McIntosh, the former leader. 'Fares Fair' − the popular name for the new fares policy − not only upset Michael Heseltine, it also got up the noses of Tory borough leaders. Especially incensed were the leaders of Bromley Council, who saw the new policy as unfair to local residents. Lacking a tube station, they hardly benefited from the new policy yet still had to pay for it.

Moved also by Ken Livingstone's growing notoriety, the Bromley leaders mounted a legal challenge against 'Fares Fair' on the grounds that it was unreasonable and unbusinesslike. Few expected Bromley to win. It had always been widely understood that the Transport (London) Act of 1969 had given the GLC wide freedom to determine the level of transport subsidy. In the event, the pundits were proved wrong. The GLC won the first round in the Division Court. But subsequently it was to lose in the Appeal Court and in the House of Lords, both unanimously declaring the fares cut and the supplementary rate unlawful, largely on the basis of a very narrow interpretation of the requirements of the Act that London transport should be run 'economically'.

Not only was this judgement of great significance for the central plank of the GLC's transport policy, it also had much wider consequences. It demonstrated the potential power of the use of the law in opposing the actions of left local councils. Since that time, Labour councils have devoted more and more resources to checking the legal foundations of their policies – largely to the benefit of the legal profession – while the threat of legal action has often been dangled by opponents. In addition, the judgement was to have a substantial impact on the overall thrust of GLC policies in the subsequent three years.

The immediate result was the need to respond. After bitter dissension on tactics within the Labour Group, and widespread confusion over what level of subsidy was lawful, the council finally agreed on 12 January 1982 to double fares, with a motley alliance of 21 Labour, three Tory and three Alliance members defeating 24 Labour opponents, including Ken Livingstone, who were pressing for defiance of the legal judgement and provoking confrontation with the government.

So, within just eight months of Labour's victory in May 1981, one of its central policies was in ruins. Round one in the battle for a radically different London had been decisively lost. At the time Mr Livingstone took a lot of the stick for the defeat. To some it was his high public profile and publicity-seeking, his diversions into external political areas, which promoted antagonism towards the GLC. Without such dabblings, it is certainly doubtful whether the challenge would ever have been brought.

The judgement, however, did not signal a total end to the GLC's transport hopes. In 1983, some 18 months after the 'Fares Fair' fiasco and after the legal ground had been thoroughly checked, the cheaper fares policy was resurrected with a new package involving a 25 per cent fares cut and a new simplified fares structure. By mid-1984, fares were roughly a fifth lower in real terms than at the time of the 1981 election.

This eventual reduction in fares was one of the main factors accounting for the GLC's sharp increase in spending. GLC cash spending rose by about 90 per cent between 1981 and 1984 compared with inflation of 20 per cent. About a quarter of this increase was accounted for by fare subsidies, about a

Fares come down. 'Just the Ticket' scheme is launched by the GLC Transport Chair Dave Wetzel, Ken Livingstone, and John McDonnell, GLC Finance Chair.

tenth by employment initiatives and about an eighth by grants to voluntary organizations.

In the Abolition White Paper, *Streamlining the Cities*, this spending increase was heavily criticized by the government. In its view the GLC and the ILEA were the two worst offenders for overspending. In 1983, the GLC's budget of £867 million was 53 per cent above the government's target of £566 million. The GLC and ILEA also accounted for some 40 per cent of the national overspend by all local authorities.

The GLC's response was that the targets were arbitrary and completely unachievable without dire consequences for London. It claimed that to achieve the target would have involved an increase in fares of 45 per cent, the abolition of pensioners' concessionary fares, an increase of council rents of £5.00 a week, an end to all grants to voluntary organizations and on spending on job creation, and the making of all administrative, professional and technical staff redundant.

This defence cut little ice with the government, who remained deeply incensed by what it saw as profligacy and deliberate provocation. Moreover, the government was especially irritated by its impotency to do anything about it. The GLC had simply ignored Whitehall's key weapon – grant penalties. It had chosen to lose all its grant and cover the loss by increasing the precept, rather than moderate spending. The government had played its last card.

In search of a role

Blatant overspending in defiance of Whitehall dictates is only one of the GLC's crimes in Mrs Thatcher's eyes. Probably more important is its overall political stance. The GLC under Ken Livingstone stands for everything the government is opposed to. The clash between Mrs Thatcher and Mr Livingstone is above all an ideological one.

In many ways, Mrs Thatcher has been less radical in practice in attempting to 'roll back the frontiers of the state' than her basic instincts would have suggested. But in local government her philosophy has led to sharp conflict. Partly this is because the cuts in public spending she has tried to impose have been concentrated on local authorities. But it is also because the move to the right at national level has coincided with a move to the left among Labour-controlled local councils. In the process Mrs Thatcher has not only confronted unexpected resistance to cuts in traditional local services. She has also faced pressure for higher spending to finance attempts to change the nature and role of local government, and to radicalize the Town Hall.

Most of the new councils which have fallen to the left were elected on detailed manifestos involving specific promises. As we have seen, the GLC's manifesto was especially comprehensive. How radical the GLC's manifesto was is debatable. Andrew McIntosh considers the 1981 manifesto to be less radical than the 1973 one, *A Socialist Strategy for London*, except in the area of employment and industrial intervention.

Perhaps a more important difference was the change in the breed of councillor, to people with a new determination to implement the commitments and a new desire for innovation.

Such determination was quickly reflected in a refusal simply to sit back and follow Whitehall instructions. The new councillors were unprepared to cut services without a fight. But the ideological divide goes much deeper than the conflict over spending levels. The new left has a different vision of the role of local councils. As well as protecting services and resisting privatization, it has set out to exploit what it views as the socialist potential of local government. This has included developing new socialist initiatives, and attempting to win popular support and build alliances around these initiatives.

This determination to change the role of local government is common to many contemporary Labour councils, but it is especially associated with the GLC. When Ken Livingstone became leader he had laid his political reputation on the line. In 1979, in the debate on the Marshall Report at County Hall, he had openly called for the abolition of the GLC.

I feel a degree of regret that Marshall did not push on and say 'Abolish the GLC', because I think it would be a major saving and would have released massive resources for more productive use.

Mr Livingstone has more recently defended this view on the grounds that from 1964 to 1981, under the fluctuating leadership of the Conservatives and 'moderate' Labour, the GLC failed to make much impact on the problems of London. Since he spent the next two years organizing the left to take control, the onus has been on him to show that his earlier judgement was misplaced and that the GLC could be converted into a model of local socialism.

In pursuing this aim, however, Ken Livingstone and his colleagues have faced considerable obstacles, which make it difficult to assess the GLC's potential as a socialist force. This is especially so in the case of the GLC's traditional strategic functions – transport, planning and housing – which have faced legal and financial barriers and an erosion of powers.

Transport illustrates particularly vividly the ideological clash between County Hall and Whitehall. Labour took control in 1981 committed to the promotion of public transport with a policy of low fares, the integration of London Transport and British Rail, new travel cards and mild constraints on the motorist. Despite the bombshell of the Bromley legal challenge, by 1984 it was able to claim some modest success, with a 20 per cent cut in fares since 1981, a 16 per cent increase in passenger usage and a 15 per cent reduction in car travel in central London. The increase in passengers was the first since the 1950s and, it is also claimed, road accidents have been reduced by 3,000 a year.

The contrast with the government's approach could hardly be sharper. In the summer of 1984, Mrs Thatcher transferred responsibility for transport from the GLC to London Regional Transport – a non-elected body responsible to the Secretary of State for Transport. The new body was required to halve its budget over the next three years. To achieve this, fares would have to rise by more than inflation in the spring of 1985, while services (that is, bus miles) and jobs would have to be cut. New plans are also afoot to privatize profitable elements of London Transport, including some bus routes.

Faced with the removal of powers and restrictions in these traditional areas, the GLC has turned to new directions. Some of these were pinpointed in the manifesto, especially the development of new economic and employment strategies. Immediately after the 1981 election, a new Industry and Employment Committee and a new Economic Policy Department were set up. This led to the establishment of GLEB – the Greater London Enterprise Board – with wide functions of financial support for existing and new firms, the establishment of new forms of public and municipal enterprise, including cooperatives, and the development of factory sites. The budget is around £30 million a year. Support has been made conditional on agreements on employment policy, on future patterns of employment and investment, and on working conditions, including wages.

These economic initiatives have been underpinned in turn by attempts to involve the community in devising and controlling projects through 'popular planning'. This has been aimed at community and workplace involvement in policy decisions – with the aim of making the economy more accountable to Londoners – and at encouraging proposals for socially useful production and services.

Another key initiative has been the establishment of vigorous equal opportunity policies. An Ethnic Minorities Committee was established with a large staff aimed at reversing the under-representation of black people in jobs, in access to some services and in the policy-making process. As well as changing internal recruitment, promotion and other practices the committee has provided grants, and attempted to raise public awareness of the problems of social discrimination through the launch of an anti-racist year in 1981.

Following the growing influence of the women's movement within the Labour movement generally, and the concern about the unequal position suffered by women, the GLC also established a Women's Committee. Among the new initiatives, this committee and its support unit have proved particularly controversial. As with the Ethnic Minorities Committee, it has had laudable aims to reduce discrimination and improve the relative position of women. Its methods, however, often received a pasting in the press.

The support unit established to service the committee was often the centre of controversy. The unit's staff was quickly expanded from three to 50 and then to 70. Most of these were specially recruited from the feminist movement outside the GLC, and many had strong views about the organization of the unit. Instead of the hierarchical approach associated with most, mostly male-dominated, workplaces, a collective approach to working was instituted. It was not long before this innovatory structure ran into problems.

These reached a head in the summer of 1984, with the press having a field day over reports of severe internal dissension within the group. This arose over ideological splits between radical and socialist feminists, over personality clashes, and over allegations of racism. A GLC internal inquiry into the unit found evidence of management inefficiency, of 'institutionalized racism' and of low morale. Subsequently, in a blaze of publicity, Louise Pankhurst, the £20,000-a-year head of the unit, left with a tax-free payment of £30,000 amidst accusations from GLC opposition members that she was 'being paid to keep her mouth shut'.

In a subsequently leaked 100-page report on the unit, Louise Pankhurst had described it as 'nightmarish'. She was especially scathing about Valerie Wise, chair of the committee, whom she claimed had continuously undermined her job. She also singled out the GLC top management for its lack of assistance, and for its general hostility to this and the other units established by the new regime.

It is not just these new policies which have irritated the GLC's opponents. They have also accused Ken Livingstone of turning the GLC into a political platform for left causes. While this is a charge which he openly accepts, he would describe it rather differently as providing a kind of alternative to parliamentary opposition, a substitute for what he has often dubbed a feeble Labour opposition in the Commons. He has also hardly denied his attempt to use the GLC as a kind of testbed for a radical Labour government, to show that radical policies can be both popular and effective.

The GLC has also unashamedly developed a new emphasis on campaigning. County Hall has been increasingly used as a wider political platform, and as a launch pad for causes as diverse as gay rights and pensioners' needs. The GLC declared 1983 a 'Peace Year', has declared London a nuclear-free zone, given support to CND and campaigned against the implementation of what it sees as useless civil defence arrangements. County Hall's vast and imposing entrance hall symbolizes this role with its widespread use of exhibitions, its extensive range of free literature and its almost continuous stream of lobbyists. Dubbed the 'People's Palace', it often looks more like the central lobby of the Palace of Westminster.

This campaigning style has been backed in turn by attempts to develop a more open and consultative approach to policy-making through public meetings and forums and the co-option of non-elected members on to committees. The Women's Committee, in particular, has attempted to involve women across London through open meetings; working parties on subjects as diverse as the police, lesbians, and violence against women; a coordinating group and eight cooptions on to the committee – four blacks, one disabled, one lesbian and two trade unionists. While those drawn in by this process have sometimes been described as unrepresentative, the approach reflects an attempt to build new alliances and mobilize popular support around radical policies.

This innovative style has hardly convinced the critics, however, who have argued that the GLC has gone beyond the boundaries of acceptable local government, and not just in the use of County Hall as a campaigning platform. The GLC has also been accused of using public money to finance its own political activity. *Politics on the Rates* is how one Tory MP and former Westminster councillor, Michael Forsyth, has described it in the title of a stinging pamphlet published by the Conservative Political Centre.

Such accusations include the appointment of prominent Labour supporters to top jobs – former left MP Reg Race to head the programme office in the GLC director-general's department and Robin Murray, a left-wing economist, to lead the economic policy group, for example. Ken Livingstone has defended such appointments on the grounds that, irrespective of their political stance, these were the best available candidates for the posts concerned. He has also argued that in the process of developing initiatives in the new policy areas such as women, ethnic minorities and economic policy, it was necessary to bring in people from outside, both in order to 'change an inherently conservative bureaucracy' and because 'we haven't got a sufficient pool of people who think in a radical and progressive way' internally.

Such politicization of bureaucracies is also not unique to left local government, even if it is usually associated with it. Some political commentators believe that it is also a characteristic of Mrs Thatcher's regimes. According to Hugo Young (the *Guardian*, 24 September 1984), 'No civil servant can rise to the top without having proved his or her positive adherence to the government's objectives' – 'a test of commitment to Thatcherism now applies with an intensity never known before' and 'extends from Whitehall far across the public service'.

The GLC has also been accused of funding its political friends through the use of grants. From 1980 to 1984 funding of voluntary organizations rose from £6 million to over £50 million. The bulk of this goes to groups which on any basis could be described as worthy and respectable. Of the total grants budget for the Women's Committee, for example, around

IN SEARCH OF A ROLE?

NEW GLC POLICY INITIATIVES 1981–1984

July 1981: ETHNIC MINORITIES COMMITTEE
● campaigns on race issues, makes grants to ethnic minority groups and projects, and monitors racism.
Budget 1983/4:   £2.9 million

July 1981: POLICE COMMITTEE
● publishes 'Policing London'
● monitors Metropolitan Police
Budget 1983/4:   £1.4 million

July 1981: ECONOMIC POLICY UNIT
● to prepare a 'London Industrial Strategy' based on alternative economic policy and 'popular planning'.
● 200 economists now on EPU staff

Summer 1981: 'Arts for People' policy statement which initiated new community arts policy

October 1981: 'FARES FAIR' – 25% cut in London Transport fares

Late 1981: Legal and Advice Centres Working Party

January 1982: GREATER LONDON TRAINING BOARD
● 'to prepare a "London Labour Plan" which would complement London Industrial Strategy'
● to fund industrial training with special help for women and ethnic minorities.
Budget 1983/4:   £6.3 million

January 1982: Gay and lesbian working party

March 1982: London declared a 'NUCLEAR-FREE ZONE'

June 1982: WOMEN'S COMMITTEE
● to fund women's projects, monitor discrimination, campaign for better nursery provision.
Budget 1983/4:   £5.9 million

September 1982:	Health Panel • to monitor NHS provision in London
December 1982:	WELFARE BENEFITS UNIT • Welfare Rights campaigning across London
1983:	Declared as 'PEACE YEAR'
Early 1983:	STRESS BOROUGHS PROGRAMME • GLC to provide aid to poor boroughs Budget 1983/4: £31.7 million
May 1983:	'JUST THE TICKET' on London Transport travelcard introduced lower fares
May 1983:	'Wheel clamping' for illegally parked cars
September 1983:	GREATER LONDON ENTERPRISE BOARD • to save jobs under threat and to create new ones. Linked with Economic Policy Unit Budget 1983/4: £31 million
September 1983:	Forum for the Elderly
1983/84:	Huge growth in grants to voluntary organizations to £47 million from £10 million in 1982/83.
1984:	Declared 'ANTI-RACIST YEAR'
May 1984:	London Consortium for Disability • to advise GLC on problems of disabled.
December 1984:	'Lorry Ban' policy to reduce heavy lorry traffic in the capital.

60 per cent goes on child care. Opponents have been upset by grants to groups such as the Greenham Common Peace Camp, the Karl Marx Library, *Spare Rib* – the radical, feminist magazine – the Gay London Police Monitoring Group and assorted peace groups such as Babies Against the Bomb.

Funding to such bodies, however, accounts for only a tiny fraction of the total grants budget. There is also nothing illegal about these GLC policies. Indeed, its lawyers have pored all over each grant to ensure that there is not. Whether it is politically unreasonable to grant aid to such bodies is clearly a matter of judgement. The Gay Police Monitoring Group, for example, receives a grant both to monitor the incidence of alleged police harassment of the gay community and to give support to its victims. Whether such a grant is considered excessively political depends on attitudes to gays and on an assessment of the extent of the problem of police harassment.

Ken Livingstone and his colleagues have certainly shaken new life into an increasingly moribund GLC. Partly this has been a response to the gradual erosion of its traditional functions. But it also reflects a new ideological commitment to reshaping local government's traditional role, which they regard as too passive and sedentary. Many of the consequent changes have been as refreshing and popular to some as they have been controversial to others. But, however the changes are judged, the GLC has certainly drifted outside the traditional framework of consensus about what legitimate local government is.

In the process, it has provided considerable political capital to its enemies. This, in turn, has been ruthlessly exploited by sections of the media and by political opponents to paint a somewhat sinister image of Ken Livingstone and his colleagues. Max Hastings of the London *Standard*, a persistent critic, has described them as a 'fungus growth of the social engineers, of the undemocratic democrats controlling vast resources and major public platforms'.

Mrs Thatcher, in turn, has rarely missed an opportunity to portray them and other left councillors in a similarly menacing light. While they may be accused of naivety, of excessive zeal, of iconoclasm, to go much further is probably taking them too seriously. Yet such images simply highlight the ideological gulf that has emerged in British politics in the early 1980s. And, in turn, they help to explain Mrs Thatcher's increasingly hostile stance towards local government in general, and the GLC in particular.

4. MRS THATCHER'S MOTIVES

Extremists are busy manipulating Labour's membership to gain power with one purpose: to impose upon this nation a tyranny which the peoples of Eastern Europe yearn to cast aside. (Mrs Margaret Thatcher, Perth, May 1981)

The government's moves to tighten central control over local government, culminating in the proposal to abolish the councillors, but not the functions, of the Greater London Council and the six English metropolitan county councils, have their roots in Mrs Thatcher's personal antipathy to local authorities, which goes back more than a decade.

In recent times the prime minister has stepped up her battles against councils for two principal reasons: she has failed to deliver anything to her supporters after a full decade of pledging to abolish, and failing that to reform, the rates; and she has seen the urban local authorities grow into formidable power bases of municipal socialism which have challenged and thwarted the assumed supremacy of the Westminster mandate.

But to understand the government's latest policies it is necessary to look, briefly, at the development of Mrs Thatcher's personal attitudes since her days as Education Secretary in Mr Heath's government of 1970–4. She immediately identified the Inner London Education Authority as everything that was undesirable in local government: not directly elected and therefore not directly accountable; very high-spending, with unfettered freedom to impose its decisions on a public which could not answer back; virtually unwinnable by the Conservative Party except in very exceptional circumstances – since 1964 the Tories have had a majority on the ILEA only in 1969–70, when Christopher Chataway was the authority's leader.

Mrs Thatcher was so appalled by the freedom of the ILEA to rate and spend to its heart's content in almost guaranteed political security that she intervened to prevent any similarly large education authorities being created anywhere else in England.

Peter Walker was busy introducing the amended reforms for urban government resulting from the 1969 Royal Commission into Local Government under Lord Redcliffe-Maud. It was these reforms which created the six English metropolitan county councils, now candidates for abolition by Mr Walker's Cabinet colleague, Patrick Jenkin. These authorities were to have been education authorities, the logic being that education should not be constrained as a function to so small a geographic area as a metropolitan district when the county covered a more sensible geographic area of urban conurbation.

Mrs Thatcher argued loudly and, ultimately, successfully that she was not prepared to have six more ILEAs under her charge with a similarly slight chance of long-running Tory political control. The smaller and more divided the better, she said. (If she had failed in this mission to stop metropolitan county education it is doubtful that the government would now be able to contemplate the abolition of the county councils.)

Once elected leader of the Conservative Party, Mrs Thatcher had to give more thought to the wider issues of local government and its constitutional relationship to central government. She never lost her distaste for the ILEA and was increasingly aware of the rising grip, through local government, of increasingly left-wing elements of the Labour Party on the major cities of the country.

In London, throughout the 1970s, Conservatives gave considerable thought and debate to the issue of whether it had been right to set up the GLC in the first place. One London MP was particularly sceptical: Geoffrey Finsberg (now Sir Geoffrey), MP for Hampstead and thus Mrs Thatcher's constituency neighbour in northern outer London. By the late 1970s he had produced his own detailed plans for axing County Hall and, as a vice-chairman of the Conservative Party, was in an influential position from which to expound his views.

Much of his support came from outer London Tories who had always been lukewarm about the GLC but, increasingly, his arguments struck a sympathetic chord in inner London too, especially in wealthy boroughs like Westminster and Kensington and Chelsea.

In one sense, the anti-GLC movement among the capital's Conservatives was merely a re-emergence of the old 'localist' traditions. But it was more than that. Increasingly, London Tories had come to see the GLC as redundant – a good enough idea in theory but one that simply had not worked out.

By the late 1970s this judgement against the GLC was by no means the exclusive property of the Conservatives. In 1977, 31 'abolitionist' candidates stood (unsuccessfully) in the GLC elections. And Labour Party spokesmen were on record as questioning whether the GLC really did enough to justify its existence. Anti-GLC feeling was particularly strong among Labour's borough councillors, reflecting their growing confidence that they could handle almost everything themselves.

As we have seen, Ken Livingstone himself called for the abolition of the GLC in March 1979, and his was not a maverick view. Leading front-bench spokesmen – respected figures like Peter Shore and Gerald Kaufman – expressed similar views around this time. So as far as London was concerned it appears that any government proposal to abolish the GLC in the late 1970s might have met with substantial cross-party approval.

Financial headaches

But Mrs Thatcher, first as party leader and later as prime minister, was always deflected from structural reforms and dragged back to one subject which reached hysteria level once a year in the form of an annual tidal wave of censorious motions at the Conservative Party conference: the rates.

Mrs Thatcher and her colleagues could rely on tumultuous ovations in response to their rhetoric about abolishing the rates, saving the ratepayers and the hard-pressed businessmen, shackling the unrestrained socialist profligates. So they presented their promises annually and enshrined them as a hostage to fortune in their general election manifestos.

Immediately after her general election success of 1979 Mrs Thatcher stunned one of her star performers in opposition, Michael Heseltine, by offering him the deeply unpopular second-rank Department of Environment in terms which made clear that nothing else was on offer. After a two-day pause for thought an unhappy Mr Heseltine accepted. Before the very first Cabinet meeting Mrs Thatcher, acutely aware that the party faithful were not expecting to pay rates for much longer, demanded 'Right. What are we going to do about local councils?'

From here the story runs like a tragi-comedy of errors. The first priority was to control council spending and rate levels while considering how to reform the finances and abolish the rates. The target was the Labour-controlled high-spending councils, which meant urban councils, the highest spenders being predominantly in inner London.

The problem was that the method of allocating central grants to councils was open-ended, meaning that the more they spent the more grant they received *automatically*. Mr Heseltine, anxious to act and eager for publicity to counter the fact that he had been given a second-rank job in a backwater department, told his civil servants he wanted a new plan and new powers immediately.

All they could offer from the dusty depths of a Whitehall drawer was a long-forgotten and rather inferior-quality scheme prepared for Peter Shore during the 1970s but never acted upon. Civil servants deserve the lion's share of the blame for the ensuing disasters. They egged Mr Heseltine on with persistently poor advice, promising that this system would give him all that he desired and more – better-targeted grant, better assessments for grant eligibility, a system of persuading high spenders to restrain themselves by a system of grant reductions for higher spending levels and, most importantly, control of local authority spending.

Ministers are heavily dependent on civil servants for advice on deeply complicated and technical matters such as this. In promising their minister far more than could ever be delivered, Environment Department officials failed Mr Heseltine grievously in 1979 and 1980.

The result was that he launched an enormous and largely unintelligible Bill – the Local Government Planning and Land Bill – into parliament. He misjudged the mood of the Commons, which reacted furiously at his attempt to cut corners and curtail the parliamentary process by introducing this hefty Bill in the Lords. He was forced to withdraw it instantly, which at least gave him the chance to delete 97 clauses and have large chunks of the remainder rewritten into English which made some sort of sense. The Local Government Planning and Land (No. 2) Bill was reintroduced in the Commons on 25 January 1980 and eventually struggled on to the Statute Book towards the year end; but the government's problems were only beginning.

This hasty attempt to control council spending through an ill-conceived and untested new method of distributing grant not only failed to curtail spending, it actually caused increases in some areas. By withdrawing grant progressively as spending rose without limiting the final level it caused rate rises to jump further and faster than they had ever done before – and the ensuing furore at party conferences was entirely predictable.

On local government finance, therefore, the government had created a new rod for its own back, and it was to be beaten mercilessly in the years up to the 1983 general election. The more it constructed lists of councils whose spending profiles were flouting the government's public expenditure philosophy, the more ministers were shown to be virtually impotent.

In fact, it was not only the perversity and inconsistency of the grant allocation system which was causing difficulty. The government was pursuing a parallel strategy of reducing the overall proportion of local government expenditure funded by central grant. This had peaked at 66.5 per cent in 1975–6 and was at 61 per cent in 1979, when Mrs Thatcher took office. It has declined steadily ever since to 51.9 per cent in 1984–5 and 48.8 per cent in 1985–6 – the latter representing £11.8 billion in grant.

These overall grant reductions are an additional factor to the grant lost through the government's various penalty regimes. The combination of factors has led to a substantial loss in grant for many councils in recent years. This has had a disproportionate effect in the urban areas – the GLC and the ILEA are among a handful of councils whose expenditure levels have excluded them totally from grant.

If the grant proportion had remained the same since 1979 and all other things had been equal, an extra 4p in the pound would have been needed on the basic rate of income tax. The effect of the grant reductions has had a great impact on London and metropolitan councils; part of the rate increases in those areas has, therefore, been due to this reduction in grant proportion which thus represents a switch between taxes – lower-than-otherwise income taxes for higher-than-otherwise local taxes. This very important conceptual change has never been properly admitted by the government; nor have the metropolitan councils and GLC effectively deployed it as a central part of their defence, arguably because it is too complicated.

Structural reforms

On the structural reform side things looked more hopeful for Mrs Thatcher in 1980. Kenneth Baker, Conservative MP for Westminster St Marylebone and eager to be a minister, produced a six-page report advocating what he knew the prime minister wanted to hear: the abolition of the ILEA. He had been asked in November 1979 by the Education Secretary, Mark Carlisle, to consider inner London's education and he concluded that it should be the responsibility of the 12 inner London boroughs in the same way as it was the responsibility, thanks to Mrs Thatcher, of the 36 metropolitan districts.

The subject was pencilled in for the 1980 Queen's Speech and many Cabinet members accepted Mr Baker's report, which said:

Local people have no direct say in the running of their local education service. ILEA prepares its own budget, determines its own expenditure and levies through the Greater London Council with a precept which cannot be effectively challenged.

He also criticized the high cost of an ILEA education – a unit cost of £631 in 1979–80 being the highest in the country, which it has been ever since, with the cost in 1984–5 being £1,441.

Mrs Thatcher and her colleagues were unhappy that the ILEA had developed into a power base which fostered 'progressive' and unorthodox teaching methods, with an alleged deleterious effect on school standards. This anxiety was fuelled by the scandal at the William Tyndale School in Islington, where an inquiry showed that many children were not acquiring the basic skills.

So there it was in 1980: estimated capital spending down to £16 million from £17.1 million in 1979, revenue spending forecast to rise to £597 million from £532 million and the cost to ratepayers rising from 43p in the pound to 54p. By 1984–5 capital had crawled back to £17 million while revenue spending was up to £973 million, requiring a rate precept of 93p in the pound.

Mrs Thatcher seemed to be on solid ground, in spite of the fact that the development of education in inner London had been built around a unified system for more than 100 years.

The moderate Labour leader of the ILEA, Sir Ashley Bramall, warned:

The first result of the break up will be total chaos in the education system in inner London. The second will be a mushrooming bureaucracy as the new education authorities will all need staff, directors of education and the like.

The third will be the creation of joint committees, as some boroughs will be unable alone to provide a full service, and if anything works against accountability it is joint committees.

Then it started to go wrong for the government. First, it was discovered that hardly any of the London boroughs had enough children to sustain an education service. Secondly, the old ratepayer problem loomed large again. Transferring education would cut the rates only in the City, Westminster and Camden. The rest would all need rate *increases* – the highest being 62.5p in Wandsworth, one of the few *Tory*-controlled boroughs in inner London.

The government hastily set up another inquiry. While it was sitting something else happened: in the 1 May 1980 local elections Labour made sweeping gains in the cities outside London (where there were no elections). More than 900 submissions were received from the public, mainly in support of the ILEA and in the end, in February 1981, the government virtually gave up by failing to come to any conclusion. The status quo won the day by default.

The worry about the rates continued, particularly in inner London where a combination of high rateable values and high-spending policies by left-wing socialists such as Ted Knight, leader of Lambeth, combined to produce howls of protest. The government's new grant and penalty scheme, intended to help the ratepayers, was simply compounding the agony. In 1981–2 inner London rate bills went up by 40 per cent.

This was all getting out of hand politically for Mrs Thatcher. After the 1979 election Mr Heseltine had set up an internal working party to look for alternatives to the rates. It worked very slowly, and in the early summer of 1980 he told it to speed up. It reported in July 1980, its confidential submission recommending either a local sales tax or a local income tax.

This plan went into the sump of complicated issues for Cabinet consideration and was supplemented in March 1981 by a proposal to peg business rates worked out by Mr Heseltine and some officials. The Cabinet again got stuck and chose the usual way out: the decision in June 1981 to publish a Green Paper on reforming the rates in the autumn, any new system not to take place until after the next general election.

Ken Livingstone ascends

Meanwhile, council spending was rising and a new dimension occurred on 7 May 1981. The Labour Party took control of the Greater London Council from Sir Horace Cutler's Conservatives. Labour took control of four metropolitan county councils and held on to the other two. They had a clean sweep of the largest local authorities in the land.

From Friday 8 May 1981, when Ken Livingstone defeated the moderate Labour leader Andrew McIntosh to become leader, abolition of the GLC – or more accurately abolition of Ken Livingstone from the world's largest local power base – forced itself repeatedly to the forefront of Mrs Thatcher's obsessions.

As the left established itself, more moderates fell by the wayside. Sir Ashley Bramall was replaced by Bryn Davies as leader of the ILEA. Mr Davies himself later fell victim to another plot and was ousted by Frances Morrell, a former adviser to Tony Benn at the Industry Department. For a time an identification with the left was sometimes more important than ability. Valerie Wise, for example, has (as we saw in Chapter 3) been criticized by some of her own colleagues as being breathtakingly short of ability as Chair of the Women's Committee. John McDonnell, on the other hand, has proved an expertly competent finance chair although he won the job on the grounds of his commitment to the far left.

The GLC began immediately to implement its programme of municipal socialism, the cornerstone of which was to revolutionize urban transport, cut fares and increase subsidy, all by increasing the GLC rate substantially. This was a major political difficulty for the government, already wrestling with the failure of its plans to curb general council spending and contemplating a Bill to limit rate rises for the Queen's Speech in the autumn of 1981.

As the left was also coming more to the fore in the metropolitan county councils, the government decided the political price was becoming too great. In June 1981 the Cabinet decided in principle to abolish the lot – GLC, ILEA and the six metropolitan county councils.

A few weeks later the Cabinet disagreed on how to limit all rate rises. Mr Heseltine and the Treasury wanted a Bill which would force a council to call a full election before it could proceed to levy a rate increase beyond a centrally determined limit. They lost to the majority of the Cabinet, who preferred a Bill to force councils to hold a referendum. The Cabinet approved this in September 1981. (The government was later forced to drop the whole of this plan after heated objections from Tory backbenchers and supplementary rates were abolished instead, mainly to save the government the embarrassment of having to drop its Bill entirely.)

Meanwhile Mr Livingstone was enraging not only the government – fuelling its eagerness to do away with him – but also some of his own party. He made what was to be the first of several forays into the controversial area of Irish politics. He was alleged, but disputed, to have refused to brand the IRA bombers in London on 10 October 1981 as criminals and to have said they were 'misunderstood'. Some of his Labour colleagues were aghast and the Tories lost no time in tabling a censure motion accusing him of 'misusing his position to further extreme views on subjects over many of which the council has no jurisdiction'. He survived that motion, but he was running into trouble. His Labour group was divided, the moderates growing increasingly annoyed with him. The left wanted him to be more extreme. His public standing was falling.

In short, it seemed that nothing would be more electorally popular than to do away with Mr Livingstone and all he represented. Mrs Thatcher took comfort in this but crucially failed to recognize that over the ensuing two years the public changed its mind.

Mr Livingstone pushed on. He approved the use of ratepayers' money for the publication of a free newspaper, *The Londoner*, to counter what he regarded as the endemic bias against the GLC of the Tory media, particularly Fleet Street. He erected a large banner at the top of County Hall proclaiming London's rising unemployment figures, an action which provoked outrage out of all proportion in the House of Commons across the River Thames. Tory MPs felt increasingly that Mr Livingstone was cocking a snook not only at the Tory government but also at the traditional supremacy of parliament.

Setbacks and gloom

On 16 December 1981 the government suffered a great setback. The long-awaited Green Paper on alternatives to the domestic rates was published, and its unmistakable conclusion was that no matter what else happened the rates would have to stay. To compound the misery, on the same day the government had to drop its Bill on rate limits and referendums and bring in its toothless replacement banning supplementary rates.

Mr Livingstone, however, was to have his share of gloom too. The next day, 17 December, the House of Lords ruled his widely popular 'Fares Fair' and the 11.9p rate which paid for it unlawful. Although he did not know it at the time, this was the beginning of Mr Livingstone's transformation from extremist menace to moderate media star. It was also the beginning of the end of his power base. The more successful he became as a national politician the more certain it was that Mrs Thatcher's personality would be unable to tolerate him.

This is not, however, how it looked in the bleak approach to Christmas 1981. The centrepiece of his policy – transport fares – was in ruins and the government was announcing, on 21 December, further cutbacks and penalties so severe that they would leave the GLC and the ILEA with no central grant at all in the next financial year.

As Mr Livingstone began 1982 with things starting to work for him, catalysed by an overtly sympathetic press over the fares fiasco, the spotlight turned back to the ILEA again. The ILEA leaders warned in February that they might raise their budget by well over £100 million to more than £800 million for 1982–3 and the precept by 16 per cent. Not only were the Tories incensed, with Mrs Thatcher privately voicing her desire to be rid of the authority, but London's Labour borough leaders also expressed fears about the electoral impact on the May 1982 local elections. In the event the ILEA made only a slight reduction, going for a £795 million budget.

This was partly responsible for the status of a paper under preparation for the Cabinet on possible means of abolition of the GLC, the ILEA and the metropolitan counties being raised to 'priority'. It is important to note here that the ILEA was again included, in spite of the Cabinet conclusion the previous year that it could not effectively be abolished. This reflects again Mrs Thatcher's determination not to give way on the ILEA: if at all possible, it had to go. In parallel, officials at the Education Department were working on a system of centralizing control of education funding by establishing a separate education grant, although this would not affect ILEA expenditure unless spending limits were also imposed.

Popular populist

Meanwhile, to the mounting horror of Conservative Party chiefs Mr Livingstone was becoming a national celebrity, as we have described in the previous chapter, better known and more easily recognized in test polls than most of the Cabinet except Mrs Thatcher – herself an uncomfortable and dismal TV performer. Very radical policies in terms of municipal employment initiatives, minority group funding and the like were still being pursued but the public had adjudged him a reasonable man, his fares policy a reasonable policy and, by implication, his rejection by the Law Lords as unreasonable.

As Mr Edward Heath was to say later during the Paving Bill debate in the Commons: who would have thought that events could turn out to mobilize public support behind Ken Livingstone?

But mobilized it was. His Irish ventures (including visits to Sinn Fein), his refusal of an invitation to the royal wedding and talk about flying black balloons from County Hall on the wedding day – even talk of a 120 per cent rate rise no longer

Daily Star 13.6.84

seemed to be enough to threaten his political power base or his popularity.

So 1983 began with Mrs Thatcher deeply unhappy about local government. She was not only being taunted from across the river by Ken Livingstone, she was now having to put up with him on national TV. In addition her first administration was clearly moving into its last phase and she had got nowhere on abolishing the rates or on local government reform. Rate bills had soared since she came to office and the left had entrenched itself throughout London, Merseyside, Manchester, and swathes of the urban north east, exploiting the municipal base for every drop of political fuel that could be squeezed.

Some of Mrs Thatcher's own colleagues were becoming uneasy about the extent to which her general view of local government and local democracy was becoming coloured by her deep-seated and almost obsessive objections to urban socialists, particularly Ken Livingstone.

Michael Heseltine, who had endured a long four years at the Environment Department, was moved to Defence in January

1983. By then he had learned from bitter experience that the civil servants in the former department were not only a good deal less clever than their Treasury counterparts but that they had an annoying habit of compensating by overselling the possibilities of many policy options. But even the civil servants had counselled him in detail against two options: trying to take absolute detailed control of local councils' finances or to abolish the GLC, the ILEA and metropolitan county councils. He accepted their reports and heeded their words.

His replacement was his long-serving and even longer-suffering deputy, Tom King. He had spent four years as local government minister of state and actually understood, in the end, the technical problems of local government finance and the grant systems. He also understood the deeply complicated implications of attempting any structural reorganization of urban government and could see no political capital to be gained. He too was against it.

Mrs Thatcher takes charge

Nevertheless, the Cabinet had so often returned to the idea that the GLC and metropolitan counties themselves were becoming anxious about their future in early 1983 – although Ken Livingstone personally was rather less interested, having determined to seek election to the Commons across the river in the general election.

Their fears were confirmed in March. The reports on rates reform and abolition had gone from officials to a committee of Cabinet ministers known as Misc 79 and chaired by the then Mr William Whitelaw, Deputy Prime Minister. In spite of the fact that the phrase 'do something' had become a central part of Mrs Thatcher's vocabulary in discussions on local government, Misc 79 had concluded that nothing could be done about the rates. But as a sop, and almost as an afterthought, it had again agreed 'in principle' to abolish the GLC and metropolitan counties. Many ministers, including Mr Whitelaw and Mr King, were confident that the sheer complexity of abolition would keep it out of policy in practice and although they were not amused by the Livingstone style they did not rate him a major electoral threat. The real issue still seemed to be the rates.

Observer 1.7.84

They reckoned, however, without Mrs Thatcher, who seemed to see Mr Livingstone as both a political and a personal threat. She set up a new committee of ministers – a subcommittee of the powerful 'E' Economic Committee – and pronounced herself chairman. She firmly accepted the abolition plans and ordered civil servants to go away and do all their work on alternatives to the rates again, concentrating on her favoured option, a local sales tax. The end of April 1983 was their new deadline.

Within weeks, in early May, the general election was announced. Although there had been a lot of debate within the party about the timing it was late in the day that the party chairman, Cecil Parkinson, finally prevailed on the prime minister to go early, in June. This meant that work towards a manifesto had to be speeded up and suddenly the issue came to a head: 'What have we got for local government?'

The real answer was nothing. The civil servants had redone their work on the rates and apart from some marginal suggestions they had finally convinced the prime minister, at least for the time being, that there were no alternatives that would do.

There was, however, a paper which Leon Brittan had concocted while Chief Secretary to the Treasury together with Robert Culpin, now Mr Lawson's press officer but then a Treasury assistant secretary in the local government finance section. This paper had been presented to Cabinet several times by Mr Brittan and rejected by all present. It argued for the government (which means the Treasury) to have the power to limit rate rises.

When reminded of the paper Mrs Thatcher immediately ordered it to be inserted in the manifesto. In spite of the caution previously expressed by other ministers about the dangers of abolition she ordered that in too, even though virtually no work had been done to examine the difficulties.

So there it was: some of the most far-reaching and un-researched proposals for local government for many years thrown into the manifesto at the last minute by Mr Parkinson at the personal behest of Mrs Thatcher. They were proposals which many Cabinet ministers had opposed time and again. As Mr Heath pointed out acidly in the Abolition Bill's second reading debate in the Commons on Tuesday 4 December 1984:

They were put in nine days after the election was called against the wishes of the Party Policy Committee. They were inserted without the general agreement of those who had been London Conservative members. The consequences are now apparent for all to see.

So sudden and surprising was their inclusion that some Cabinet ministers claimed afterwards that they had no idea until the last second that they were in. Mr Heseltine was reported to be 'dismayed' and Mr King, when first told the news by an aide on a train in northern England, was said to have been shaken and 'aghast'. He had, as Local Government Minister and Environment Secretary, spent four years arguing against these very ideas.

But Mrs Thatcher was unconcerned. She was seeking the support of the entire electorate for permission to intervene to stop the expensive spending of socialist ideologues in the cities. And she was to abolish a layer of socialist government, prin-cipally the Greater London Council. No matter that the ILEA, her *bête noire*, was to survive. No matter that it might be difficult and contentious.

Supreme in her thinking was the final realization of what had become a personal challenge: the removal of the power base which had enabled Ken Livingstone to taunt and defy her, to rival and, in some ways, even to better her. Even if he slipped into parliament (which he ultimately failed to do) a repeat performance would be impossible. And if he did not she could and would wipe him off the national political map.

5. PAVING THE WAY

It immediately lays the Conservative Party open to the charge of the greatest gerrymandering of the last 150 years of British history. (Edward Heath, House of Commons, 11 April 1984)

Having decided to abolish the GLC, included it in the manifesto and then decisively won the general election in June 1983, the next unavoidable question for Mrs Thatcher was how to do it.

The first move in the process of abolition was the establishment of an *ad hoc* Cabinet subcommittee to draw up a detailed timetable and plans. Called the Ministerial Group on the Abolition of the GLC and the Metropolitan County Councils, and codenamed MISC 95, it was chaired by the new Secretary of State for the Environment, Patrick Jenkin. The appointment of Mr Jenkin must now look like a major error of judgement by Mrs Thatcher. But at the time she had limited options.

The two previous Environment Secretaries, Michael Heseltine and Tom King, had strongly indicated their opposition to abolition, and to Mrs Thatcher's other key local government manifesto commitment, ratecapping, in earlier Cabinet discussions. Other senior ministers had also shown little stomach for the idea. Patrick Jenkin, on the other hand, was not known to have strong views on either subject. In addition, as a former Social Services and Industry Secretary, and wanting and expecting to be appointed Chancellor of the Exchequer, he had to be given a senior post. He also had a reputation for hard work, loyalty and, as a lawyer, an important ability to grasp details.

Against this Mrs Thatcher might have been warned by Mr Jenkin's equal reputation for an inability to communicate, for blunders, and for smugness. This dates from his notorious advice to the nation to brush its teeth in the dark during the long winter blackouts of the 1973 miners' strike. As it was to turn out, Mr Jenkin's qualities were also to prove no match against Mr Livingstone. Against the GLC leader's relaxed, disarming style and rough charm, Mr Jenkin simply looked clumsy and leaden-footed. Having hoped for and expected the chancellorship, he was also a bitterly disappointed man.

The role of Misc 95

The Cabinet committee met in the immediate aftermath of the Tories' overwhelming election victory. This and several subsequent meetings were to have a decisive effect on the future course of events. The decisions of the committee were revealed

FARE WARNING

This newspaper backs the Government plan to abolish the metropolitan councils (including the GLC).

But we recognise – as should Tory Ministers – that it is by no means self-evident to most men and women living in these areas that they stand to benefit from the change.

As opinion polls indicate, they are going to take a lot of convincing.

The best way to do that is to prove to the commuting public that dispensing with Red Ken and his ilk will not mean fewer buses, fewer trains and higher fares.

'Anything they can do we can do as cheaply and more efficiently' – that should be the Tory slogan.

But the man on the Clapham omnibus is not going to believe it unless Tory Ministers, in turn, start believing that good public transport is a virtue ... not a necessary evil.

Daily Mail, 27.3.84

HOW CAN YOU STOP ELECTIONS?

... people have rumbled the real reason behind the Government's determination to eliminate the GLC and the other metropolitan councils – which is, that when faced with an obstacle it finds politically inconvenient, it will do all that it can to steamroller it out of the way. As one GLC member put it yesterday: 'The Prime Minister cannot tolerate London remaining a base of a political group opposed to her. It is simply too powerful a base for opposition.' And he is a Conservative.

... Ministers were reported this weekend to be pained and resentful at growing suggestions that there is a dangerously authoritarian streak in this Government. But if they wonder how such thoughts get about, they need only to glance back through their recent record, and in particular to ponder the sort of priorities implicit in the way their debate about the future of the GLC and the metros was resolved.

Guardian, 27.3.84

OFF WITH THEIR HEADS

It is not usual to think of Mrs Thatcher's as a weak Government. But certainly in the case of its ill-thought-out plans to abolish the GLC and the six metropolitan counties it is displaying all the stubbornness and perversity normally associated with far more vulnerable administrations.

The truth is that, in terms of local government, London was always a special case. Unlike the metropolitan counties, it was not an artificial creation: in the minds of its electors, even those who may choose to live in the suburban outskirts but largely work in the capital itself, it remains a living entity.

London is one of the great cities of the world – and that, unlike Paris, New York or (even today) Washington, it should be stripped of having any directly elected governing authority of its own is not only an offence against democracy: it is a denial of the capital's dignity and history.

Observer, 15.4.84

SCRAP THEM

A West Indian pre-school group is to receive a £139,000 grant from the Greater London Council.

It has just 20 pupils – so the grant works out at almost £7,000 each child.

Why is the GLC wasting money trying to persuade people that it should be spared from Margaret Thatcher's axe when its own foolish antics make the case for abolition ever stronger?

Hurry up, Maggie!

Sun, 25.4.84

BATTLE FOR MINDS

The Government should have had little trouble winning the propaganda battle surrounding its proposed local government reforms.

These measures – rate capping and the abolition of the GLC and the metropolitan councils – are designed overall to reduce the burden of local government on the ratepayers and taxpayers.

Can it really be possible to lose on this wicket?

'Yes' seems to be the answer.

Both the GLC leader, Mr Ken Livingstone, and the Metropolitan councils, have run rings round Environment Secretary Mr Patrick Jenkin in the propaganda war.

Mr Livingstone does not even bother to conceal his contempt for his ratepayers. His latest wheeze is to give £16,000 to a female 'pop group' so that they can make a record attacking Mrs Thatcher and supporting the GLC's campaign against abolition.

He turns out ammunition like this every other day. But all Mr Jenkin and his team have done with it has been to shoot the Government in the foot.

Daily Express, 21.5.84

HOT STUFF, KEN

Even though they dislike Ken Livingstone, many Tories grudgingly admit that he is a brilliant campaigner.

His fight against the abolition of the GLC has been watched with admiration by experts in the art of political propaganda.

Saatchi and Saatchi, the top Tory publicity outfit, could hardly have done better.

At almost every turn he has outwitted the Government in the fight to win public support to his cause.

One Tory true-blue, after meeting him for the first time, commented: 'What a charming chap. I always thought he was a monster.'

Sunday Mirror, 1.7.84

in two minutes from Patrick Jenkin to the prime minister which were subsequently leaked to the *Guardian* and the *Financial Times* several months later in March 1984, a few days before the publication of the Paving Bill which was to cancel the elections due in May 1985. It was widely rumoured at the time that the leak came directly from 10 Downing Street. Some of the potential problems with the strategy agreed had begun to emerge and Mrs Thatcher may well have wanted to cover herself by at least partially dissociating herself from these strategies. Certainly no leak inquiries were launched.

In the committee, it was agreed that abolition and the transfer of functions could not take place until 1 April 1986, nearly three years away. Because of its complexity, the main abolition legislation could not itself be introduced until the 1984/5 session of parliament. This timetable, however, was to create what was to subsequently prove a very serious hole in the government's strategy. The GLC and the metropolitan county council elections were due in May 1985, eleven months before the councils were due to be abolished, and before the Abolition Bill itself was likely to become law.

The government had three choices for dealing with this problem. First, to let the elections proceed but limit the life of the new council to eleven months. Second, to cancel the elections and let the existing administration continue in office for the remaining eleven months. Third, to cancel the elections and substitute an interim body to run the GLC and preside over the devolution of the functions until abolition took effect.

The minutes reveal that at first, the second option was the front runner in Mr Jenkin's mind. He was then planning legislation to allow the existing administrations at the GLC and the metropolitan counties – all of which were then Labour-controlled – an extra year of office. This option, however, created the appalling dilemma that it would have left 'Red Ken' in power for another year, and would have been difficult to explain and defend to Conservative backbenchers and supporters – who after all saw abolition as a way of silencing Ken and ending his antics, not extending them.

Over the course of the summer, backbenchers, especially from London constituencies, appalled at the prospect of giving Mr Livingstone another year in office, appear to have successfully lobbied Mr Jenkin to reconsider the idea. By the autumn, Mr Jenkin's thinking had changed. He was still opposed to the elections proceeding, for fear that they might turn into a referendum on abolition. A Labour victory on an anti-abolition platform would cause considerable political embarrassment for the abolition strategy, as would even a Tory victory given the opposition of Tory GLC members to abolition. As his minute of 20 September to the prime minister reveals:

The Group are agreed that [the 1985 elections] cannot be allowed to go ahead: other objections apart, abolition would be a major issue in the elections, so that there would be a major public debate going on after the House of Commons had voted for Second Reading of the Abolition Bill.

The meeting then considered the two remaining options for replacing the elections: 'deferral', with the existing councillors remaining in office, and 'substitution', with councillors appointed by the boroughs taking over the role of the GLC after the election date. The views of the group on these options were divided.

Some members argued that there were constitutional and political objections to substitution: in particular, that we should be accused of creating a new procedure in order to engineer a change in political control in the GLC area and possibly (depending on the results of elections between now and May 1985 and on the basis of selection of the substitute councillors) some of the Metropolitan County Council (MCC) areas.

A small majority of the Group, however, considered that both our own supporters and the wider public would find it incomprehensible that we should, in effect, extend the terms of office of the GLC and the MCCs. Moreover, to do so would provide those bodies with scope of obstruction at a time when this would be most damaging to our policies. They therefore favoured substitution.

In the minute, Mr Jenkin went on to describe this decision as 'probably one of the most [politically] sensitive decisions we have to take', a statement which later was to have such a bitter ring of truth. He then went on to recommend the substitution option to Mrs Thatcher and the Cabinet. Initially Mrs Thatcher indicated her opposition to this strategy. In another minute (also leaked) from her private secretary, Michael Scholar, to Mr Jenkin's private secretary, John Ballard, it was indicated that 'The Prime Minister prefers deferment of the May 1985 elections of the GLC and MCCs to substitution.' Subsequently she chose to fall in line with Mr Jenkin's preference for substitution, and it was this option which was included in the subsequent White Paper *Streamlining the Cities*, published on 7 October 1983.

It was this tactical decision which was to haunt Mrs Thatcher and Mr Jenkin time and time again in the ensuing process of implementing the abolition manifesto commitment. Subsequently, Mrs Thatcher was to rue the day she failed to abide by her own instincts and overrule the Jenkin strategy.

The 'Paving' Bill

The Bill – the Local Government (Interim Provisions) Bill – which provided for the cancellation of the elections and the substitution of borough and district councillors was published on 30 March. Few Bills in recent memory have had such a stormy ride through parliament.

There were three elements which were to prove especially contentious because of their wider constitutional implications.

First, the cancellation of the elections for a body which had not yet been abolished was unprecedented. Second, the effect of the decision to establish an interim body from May 1985 to run the GLC, made up of councillors appointed by the London boroughs, was to change the political control of the GLC from Labour to Conservative. This was because a minority of the 32 London boroughs were in Labour hands. Third, the Bill provided that the provision to cancel elections was not automatic but would be 'triggered' only on the second reading of the main Abolition Bill in the Commons. In effect this eliminated the vote of the Lords, since it assumed that the Lords would endorse the view of the Commons.

The potential problems with the Bill were signalled as early as the second reading in the Commons on 11 April. Already, in a letter to *The Times* on 10 April, ten Conservative GLC members had raised their disquiet about a change in political control created by Act of Parliament. As the authors of the letter put it:

To turn this matter on its head, we ask your readers to consider what would have been the reaction if the Conservatives were in control at County Hall and the present proposals were emanating from a government under the leadership of the far left.

It was this element of the proposals which was, above all else, to dog the course of the Bill in the subsequent months.

Although known for his unsympathetic stance towards government policies in many areas, Edward Heath, the former prime minister, delivered an especially critical broadside during the Commons' debate on the second reading, describing the Bill as a

bad Bill, and paving the way for a worse Bill. It is bad because it is a negation of democracy ... Worst of all is the imposition by parliamentary diktat of a change of responsible party in London government. There cannot be any justification for that.

He added: 'It immediately lays the Conservative Party open to the charge of the greatest gerrymandering in the last 150 years of British history.' Mr Heath was joined in this rebellion by other ex-Cabinet ministers including Mrs Thatcher's old political enemies, Ian Gilmour and Francis Pym. Mr Pym commented in the debate: 'The imposed change of party political control in these circumstances will cause the government and this party no end of trouble. It isn't worth it, the price is too high.'

In the event, the government had an impregnable majority to call on, and the Bill was given a second reading by 301 votes to 208, a majority of 93. Even so, Mr Heath and 18 other Tories voted against the government, a warning of what was to come. It was also extremely damaging to the government's reputation to have Tories of the status of Mr Heath, Mr Pym and Mr Gilmour declaring such open defiance against a key element of the government's programme.

The government's defence against these charges was that it would have been pointless and expensive to hold the elections and that there were precedents for the cancellation of elections to bodies that were due for abolition during the reform of local government. This was so when London government was reformed in 1964, establishing the GLC, and also in England and Wales in 1972. However, that was where the government's case ended. There were no precedents for the cancellation of elections for a body that was not yet abolished. Nor were there precedents for the substitution of a nominated for an elected council, and so no previous cases of a change in political control by such a move.

Mr Jenkin's response was that there was no precedent for the proposals because there was no precedent for the situation. Unlike the situation in previous reorganizations, the councils to which the functions of the abolished councils would be transferred were already in existence, and ministers therefore argued that it was appropriate for the interim body to be made up of nominees from these successor councils rather than extending the life of the existing ones.

In addition they were concerned that if granted a reprieve, the existing GLC would be able to carry out obstructive policies. Mr Jenkin spoke of the prospect of 'chaos and confusion' if the process of abolition was left in the hands of the existing administration. Whether this would have proved so or not – and the Paving Bill itself contained a number of measures designed to prevent obstruction – a change of party control by fiat was to prove a high price to pay to avoid such a prospect.

Moreover the constitutional issue was not the only concern over 'substitution'. There was widespread anxiety about the likely effectiveness of the proposed substitute council, which was to be composed of councillors nominated by London's 32 boroughs. Major doubts were raised by GLC and borough councillors of both parties about whether the proposed interim body would be up to the running of the GLC for a year while preparing for the handover of its services. Such concern was expressed by both supporters and opponents of abolition. Councillor Bernard Brooke-Partridge, long-standing Tory GLC member and former chairman of the GLC, speaking on 'The London Programme', was particularly concerned about the ability of the nominated councillors to do the job of managing the GLC in the interim year and preparing for the devolution of functions.

I don't think that they're going to be of adequate calibre for the job. I prophesy enormous problems for them. I'm almost sorry for them really because they won't even know where the loos are. They really are in for a terribly bad time. I've been here 17 years and I can quite confidently tell you that it took me six to nine months to find my way around this building and to know who you really telephone and who you really speak to if you want to get something done.

Similar concern was voiced by devoted advocates of abolition such as Peter Bowness, leader of Croydon Council and leader of the London Boroughs Association. He had advocated the appointment of a commission to run the council's services for the necessary eleven months. Peter Bowness and Lady Porter, leader of Westminster Council, had told the Conservative Party local government conference that the government's proposals would not work and that the devolving of the functions from the GLC to the boroughs should be handled by a government-appointed commission which would act like a liquidator. Shirley Porter told Mr Jenkin, 'There is no point in worrying about being accused of being dictatorial. Nobody loves you anyway. Get on with the job and do it properly.'

These arguments carried little weight with opponents of the

government's strategy. Mrs Thatcher's worst fears were confirmed as opposition within her own ranks continued to become more and more vocal. Worse still for the government was the effect it was to have on the popularity of Ken Livingstone. If the government had instead opted for extending the life of the expiring councils it is unlikely that such opposition would have been unleashed.

'Say No to No Say'

It was not simply the government's own inept handling of the issue which was to turn the tide of popular opinion against it. From March onwards, the GLC mounted an imaginative and decisive campaign against the decision to cancel the elections. Unlike Mrs Thatcher's abolition plans, the GLC's campaign strategy was elaborately prepared well in advance of the publication of the Paving Bill. Target groups from MPs and peers to councillors and industrialists, and interest groups such as grant-aided organizations and pensioners, were identified. Attempts to influence these groups took the form of individual lobbying, special events and advertising. To conduct the advertising campaign the advertising agents – Boase Massimi Pollitt, veterans of campaigns for the Labour Party and NALGO, and architects of the 'Keep it Local' campaign of the Association of Metro-

The attempt to abolish the GLC elections, due to be held in 1985, was depicted as a frontal attack on democracy in this GLC poster. The message was strong and hard to forget.

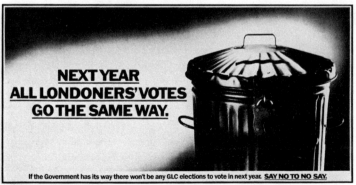

NEXT YEAR ALL LONDONERS' VOTES GO THE SAME WAY.

If the Government has its way there won't be any GLC elections to vote in next year. SAY NO TO NO SAY.

This GLC poster aimed itself at MPs and peers debating the Paving Bill. Could the cradle of democracy be party to a plan to destroy democracy in London? The point was telling.

politan Authorities – were appointed in mid-February.

The issues that were thought most likely to raise public anxiety were thoroughly researched and it was decided to home in on the constitutional issues raised by the scrapping of the elections. From mid-March, to coincide with the publication of the Paving Bill, the first 'Say No to No Say' – the clever campaign slogan – posters began to surface. Soon London was littered with GLC posters using slick and evocative slogans and powerful images. With their own public relations advisers, the GLC was playing Mrs Thatcher at her own game.

One poster portrayed a mass of red tape with the caption, 'What will London be like without the GLC?' Another showed a picture of parliament, asking 'What kind of place is it that takes away your right to vote and leaves you with no say?' One showed a padlocked dustbin, labelled 'Next year all Londoners' votes will go the same way'. Just as Mrs Thatcher's earlier Saatchi-and-Saatchi-devised campaign had aimed at the Labour vote, so the GLC advertising was concentrated in the pro-Tory tabloids – the *Sun*, the *Daily Mail* and the *Daily Express*. 'Broadly speaking, the more hostile the editorial stance of the paper, the more likely we would be to advertise', says Tony Wilson, the GLC public relations head.

As it became clear that the campaign was beginning to work, there were abortive attempts to fight back. According to *Marketing* (28 June 1984), there was talk of using Saatchi for a retaliatory spree. There was much talk of 'misuse of public funds' – the advertising campaign alone cost £3 million – in the press and among Tory backbenchers. One Conservative MP, Angela Rumbold, tabled a Private Member's Bill to try to have the advertising banned. Neither proposal came to anything.

Some anti-Livingstone pundits accused him of hypocrisy in defending democracy. In response to the defend GLC slogan 'If you want me out you should have the right to vote me out', the *Daily Express* commented (30 April 1984), 'The trouble is that Londoners never had the chance to vote Red Ken *in* as their leader', in reference of his toppling of Andrew McIntosh the day after the elections. The GLC, meanwhile, defended its campaign, and its cost, by arguing that it dealt with constitutional, not political issues and that its cost to the average

Londoner was only 0.33p a week.

While the precise success of the campaign is difficult to gauge, opinion certainly shifted. This shift was partly due to concern about the principle of abolition as well as the means chosen by the government. Opposition mounted among professional groups such as planners and architects, among Conservative GLC members, and among leading Conservatives who were worried about the technical problems of abolition and leaving London without a voice. But opposition was fuelled too by the government's handling of the matter, which was widely felt to be extraordinarily clumsy, and the improving public profile of Ken Livingstone himself.

Whatever the root cause, the public were strongly opposed to abolition. In a MORI poll in the *Standard* at the end of March 1984, 61 per cent of Londoners were against abolition and only 22 per cent for. This compares with 54 per cent against and 22 per cent for in a similar poll in October 1983. By the summer of 1984, opposition had reached 74 per cent. Worse still for the government, Mr Livingstone's image had been transformed. A year previously a MORI/*Standard* poll found 58 per cent of Londoners dissatisfied with him and only 26 per cent satisfied. By March 1984, the number dissatisfied had fallen to 42 per cent and the number satisfied risen to 43 per cent. Ken Livingstone had been changed, in the words of the *Guardian*, 'from popular demon to defender of democracy against dictatorial central government' (8 June).

The campaign itself may have swung public opinion behind Mr Livingstone and against Mrs Thatcher, but it had no impact on the passage of the Bill through the Commons. Despite Tory rebel opposition, the Bill passed with a safe majority. But there was still a major hurdle to overcome before the controversial Bill was to pass into law. It had to proceed through the House of Lords. And it had always been clear that the government would have a much stickier time in the second chamber. The second reading of the Bill in the Lords took place on Monday 11 June. In the preceding week, there was intense lobbying on both sides.

The GLC's 'self-defence' campaign budget had not been spent only on advertising. It was also used to employ professional lobbyists. Roland Freeman, a former Tory GLC member who had switched to the SDP, was appointed as a full-time lobbyist to woo the Lords. He had built up a card index of the biographical details and political interests of every member of the House of Lords. In a parallel campaign, the metropolitan counties had employed a professional lobbying company – GJW Ltd – founded by former Conservative, Labour and Liberal political advisers.

The rise of the peers

Together these lobbyists set about convincing peers of the case against the government. As the Bill's first stage in the Lords drew nearer, the lobbying – including receptions for peers at County Hall – intensified on both sides. Viscount Whitelaw, leader of the House of Lords, and 'Bertie' Denham, the government chief whip, were making furious efforts to cajole loyal peers from all over Britain to Westminster to defend the government.

The system of 'whipping' in the Lords is wholly different from that in the Commons, where MPs are obliged by a combination of instructions and threats to toe the party line. In the Lords, the system is much more casual. Less active peers tend to attend as a favour or out of a sense of duty, and can react with hostility to pressure. The whips on both sides use the 'old boy network' and mild pressure – gentlemanly tactics – to get their vote out on critical occasions. Bertie Denham in particular is renowned for his ability to charm peers into the chamber. Such a haphazard system means that votes on contentious issues are much more unpredictable. This was even more the case on the occasion of the second reading of the Paving Bill.

Only on rare occasions – traditionally only once or twice a year – does the chief whip in the Lords resort to issuing a three-line whip. Even then up to 40 per cent of peers, especially on the Tory side, never attend. To get a majority for other Bills, Lord Denham had already issued two such three-line whips in that session. The second reading of the Paving Bill became the third. For some peers, this was overstepping the mark. During the debate on that Monday evening one Conservative peer, Lord Mountgarret, protested that 'extreme pressure' had been brought to bear by the whips on Tory peers to support the government, and urged peers not to be 'steam-rollered'.

Not only was intense lobbying taking place, there was also a rare collusion over tactics between the opposition parties. Convention in the Lords decrees that Bills are not defeated on second reading. Dissent with the principle of the Bill is shown by the tabling of an amendment critical of but not actually wrecking it. Labour and Alliance peers – both committed to defeating the Bill – had buried their differences over tactics and tabled a joint motion describing it as 'a dangerous precedent'. While this of itself would not have destroyed the Bill, such a strongly worded amendment would have been a serious blow to the government if passed, and it would have been under serious pressure to withdraw or amend.

The amendment's wording was cleverly designed to try and maximize the support of crossbenchers and dissident Tories. As the day of the second reading drew nearer, there was wide-spread speculation about the outcome of the vote. On paper, the Tories have a decisive majority in the Lords with about 450 peers taking the Tory whip, 110 Labour, 80 Alliance and around 200 crossbenchers. These figures, however, mean less in practice because of erratic attendance and the unpredictability of crossbench opinion. But signs that the government could be in for a close fight came on the Friday before the debate when Lord Plummer, a Tory peer and former GLC leader, had declared on BBC Radio 4's 'World at One' that he was consider-ing voting for the amendment:

I must say, I have a very severe conscience about it. I think that I may have to vote against this Bill as I think a number of other Conservative peers will do also.

This was the first indication of a possible break in Tory ranks and, along with the Tory opposition in the Commons, it may have helped to influence the subsequent voting.

The evening of the second reading saw the highest attendance since 28 October 1971, when the Lords voted on the principle of Britain joining the Common Market. In contrast with the Commons, debates in the Lords are usually quiet and deferential; heckling is frowned upon. Yet the vote at ten o'clock followed an untypically lengthy and heated debate with 39 speakers, constant interruption by opposition peers and persistent intervention by the Speaker. Summoned from their country homes and city offices, peers were there who had not been seen for years. The debate was recorded live and, probably overcome with their sudden rise to prominence, the peers rose to a rare eloquence, quoting Shakespeare, the Bible, Milton and Keats.

The debate was dominated by the constitutional issues involved. The government faced a barrage of criticism over the introduction of the Bill in advance of the main legislation to abolish the councils. Lord Hailsham time and again had his earlier expressed view about an 'elective dictatorship' thrown back at him. Lord Hooson, a Liberal peer who moved the amendment, argued that the House of Lords was on trial in its role as the guardian of the constitution, and urged peers to place their constitutional duty above party allegiance.

A constant theme was that the Bill was a threat to the authority of the Upper House. This was because the cancellation of the elections through the Bill was to be triggered on the second reading of the main Abolition Bill in the Commons rather than the Lords, thereby rendering the vote of the Lords virtually redundant. The strong views expressed were not necessarily in opposition to the principle of abolition itself but to the *means* adopted, and what was seen as the dangerous constitutional precedent being set.

At ten the debate ended and the vote was taken. In the quaint custom of the Lords, those voting for the amendment filed through the 'content' lobby while those against went through the 'non content' lobby. As the vote was awaited a hush fell over the packed chamber, with peers crowded around the throne and MPs and visitors packing the public gallery. It was like the state opening of parliament.

The vote, when it came, was a surprise above all to the government whips. The government survived by a mere 20 votes, the amendment attacking the Bill falling by 217 to 237. Given the rarity with which governments are defeated in the Lords on a critical amendment at second reading, this was rightly and widely interpreted as a major embarrassment. In the ensuing debate Lord Whitelaw attempted to put a brave face on the outcome, but it was clear that he was shaken by the strength of feeling against the Bill and the narrowness of the vote. While the government was able to claim a victory, it was widely viewed by the press, the opposition and some supporters as little more than Pyrrhic.

This became even clearer when the voting breakdown emerged the next day. Despite the vigour of the whipping exercise, seven Conservative peers voted with the opposition and 29 abstained. Moreover the majority, slender as it was, was heavily dependent on the votes of hereditary peers, who are the least democratic element of the chamber. Of the government's 237 votes, 178 came from hereditary peers, 59 from life peers, and none from the bishops. The opposition vote, in contrast, was dominated by 187 life peers, with seven bishops and only 59 hereditary peers. In addition, the government got only limited support from crossbenchers, who have traditionally tended to support it on key votes on the principle of legislation. Of the 200 or so crossbenchers more than 40 voted for the opposition amendment and only 22 backed the government.

In the days following the vote, speculation mounted as to whether the government could now get the Bill through the Lords. The second reading was merely the opening stage and the one when peers are traditionally reluctant to defeat the government. It was the committee stage, due next and taken on the floor of the House, which would prove decisive. The government was faced with a difficult choice: to concede defeat and amend the Bill so that it would survive, or soldier on and risk the chance of further humiliation in the hope of getting it through unscathed.

The latter course was adopted. The government inevitably claimed it foresaw no difficulties in getting the legislation through. The key issue, however, was how many Tory peers the whips could 'charm' back into the Lords and into the government lobbies. So the lobbying continued on both sides.

The defeat

The committee stages were set to follow some two and a half

WHAT THE PAPERS SAID ABOUT THE PAVING BILL BEFORE ...

RIGHT TO VOTE

Parliament is soon to be asked to strip the right to vote from more than five million Londoners. The request comes in the shape of a Bill from the Environment Secretary, Mr Patrick Jenkin, seeking to abolish the GLC elections due on May 2 next year. That is intended as the first step towards doing away with the Greater London Council itself, which will come in a second and much bigger Bill which will not be published until the end of this year.

And there lies the problem. In a democracy, to cancel an election is perhaps the most serious step a Government can take. It has not been done in this country this century except in war-time. Mr Jenkin's nationwide plans, which include the six big metropolitan counties, would disenfranchise more than 13 million voters.

... In particular, there has been a growing tide of opinion that, even after the GLC empire has gone, the capital must keep some kind of elected, London-wide authority.

Anyone who thinks these are frivolous objections might try to imagine the Tory hullabaloo if Mr Tony Benn, as a Labour minister, were to suggest ditching an election. Mr Jenkin can proceed with confidence (his and ours) only when his case is cast-iron. At the moment, it falls worryingly short of that.

Standard, 1.3.84

A POLITICAL EXPEDIENT

... The plan to pave the way for abolition by cancelling local elections has been widely criticized, not least by some of the Government's most senior backbenchers. The measure, known as the Local Government (Interim Provisions) Bill, is another illustration of the tangle in which the Conservative Administration has ensnared itself over local government.

Since the 1979 general election the Government has persistently run into difficulties on this front. This is partly because of its inability to develop a coherent strategy for structural and financial reform. The Government has also tended to rush legislation into Parliament to secure its ends without giving careful enough thought to the means.

... Shadow body

The cancellation of elections on the due date seems designed to avoid the possibility of an embarrassing result for the Government and an equally embarrassing debate while the abolition proposals are being examined in Parliament.

... On balance, therefore, it is a pity that the Local Government (Interim Provisions) Bill has been published at all. It would be preferable for the 1985 elections to take place in the usual way and, if Parliament approves abolition, to allow the threatened but still elected councils to run down and expire on the appointed day.

Financial Times, 11.3.84

THE 'PAVING BILL' IN THE LORDS

... Distaste

It is probably not now possible for the elections to take place because the traditional role of the House of Lords is to amend and improve legislation rather than to destroy and dismiss.

But the Lords can do two things. First, when it considers the Bill line by line it can still stop the cancellation of the 1985 elections and opt for leaving the existing elected councillors in place until abolition is enacted.

Secondly, it can make clear to the Government its distaste for this sort of approach to local elections.

A Liberal peer, Lord Hooson, has tabled a 'reasoned amendment' which would add to the motion 'that the Bill be now read a second time' the following rejoinder: 'but this House regards the Government's introduction of this Bill as unnecessary; notes that it was not proposed in the Conservative Party's election manifesto, and considers it an ill-judged attempt to institute non-representative, non-elected bodies and clothe them with the powers of properly elected and constituted councils, and, further, to do so before Parliament has had the opportunity of deciding whether the Greater London Council and the metropolitan councils should be abolished.'

Such a rebuke deserves support from all sides.

Financial Times, 5.6.84

VOTE FOR DEMOCRACY

Defenders of the House of Lords say it exists to prevent the House of Commons getting too big for its boots.

Those who want to abolish it say it is the last bunker of the Conservative party.

Today, we have the chance to find out who is right.

The Lords are due to debate a Bill, sent to them by the Commons, whose purpose is to scrap next year's elections for the Greater London Council.

Instead, the GLC, for the last year of its life, would be run by local councillors chosen from London boroughs. Overnight, control of the GLC will switch from Labour to Tory.

All without an election.

This is a blatant piece of political gerrymandering born of the Government's hatred for Ken

Livingstone. The Commons and the Cabinet should be ashamed of themselves.

Labour and Alliance peers have attached an amendment to the Bill which would condemn it. But because of the built-in, hereditary Tory majority, the amendment can only be passed with the support of rebel Tory peers.

It should get it. The Lords, even though unelected, should tell the Government that it goes too far when it tries to abolish elections for others.

Daily Mirror, 11.6.84

IMPROVING THE PAVING BILL

... The concession that must be made is over the so-called interim arrangements for administering the metropolitan counties and the GLC in 1985–86. The local government franchise is, it has to be said, a debased system of election, marred by a prevalent apathy and a disconnexion between fiscal incidence and ballot box preference. But that is no reason for the contempt of local electoral choice contained in the paving bill's provision for replacing the set of councillors elected to the GLC and the counties with an unwilling gang of nominees from organizations with a different electorate and separate purposes.

Times, 11.6.84

ODD BEDFELLOWS

... Whether the champions of liberty in the Lords will succeed in emasculating this Bill through a series of amendments remains to be seen. The lives of Conservatively inclined backwoodsmen will certainly be agitated over the coming months, for the Government will have to rely upon their loyal votes in order to withstand the massed ranks of Labour, Alliance, crossbencher and Tory rebel peers. Some dusty Lords will be bussed in from distant parts. But if there are substantial amendments, we may look forward with confidence to the prospect of Mr Livingstone and indeed of Mr Kinnock making stirring and even tearful reference to the enlightened character of the Upper House. When these amendments are sent back to the Commons Labour cannot fail to pay tribute to the 'undemocratic' Chamber which, in a moment of aberration, it unequivocally undertook in its 1983 General Election Manifesto 'to abolish ... as quickly as possible'.

Daily Telegraph, 13.6.84

THE BENEFIT OF SECOND THOUGHTS

Once again the House of Lords demonstrates its value as the place for second thoughts.

By giving the Government a tiny majority of 20 on the Bill to abolish Greater London Council elections next year it sends a warning signal to No. 10: Be very careful about tampering with the democratic process.

The argument for doing away with the useless, costly GLC and the other metropolitan dinosaurs is overwhelming.

But the case for abandoning a scheduled election is much less clear-cut.

Daily Express, 13.6.84

PAVED WITH BAD INTENTIONS

... The only argument originally against extending the life of the GLC was the alleged unpopularity of Red Ken. But circumstances have changed. Mr Livingstone is now the doughty defender of democracy, and the damage the government is inflicting upon itself by prolonging the row far outweighs the always dubious justification of keeping Mr Livingstone in office for a few months. So if it is such an obvious escape route, why has the government not made this concession already? The answer probably lies in the overweening pride of Mrs Thatcher. All the signs are that it is her personal obstinacy, her refusal to contemplate being seen to give in to pressure, even when this is to her own political advantage, that lie behind governmental inflexibility.

Guardian, 13.6.84

ABOLISH THIS BAD ABOLITION BILL

... What worries Mrs Thatcher is that if she allows the election to go ahead it will be used by the Labour Party as a referendum on the whole abolition issue. Worse still, they would use vast amounts of ratepayers' money to propagandize their cause.

There can be no doubt that this is what would happen and it would be very undesirable. But the alternative route which is being taken by the Government is even worse.

What an appalling precedent is being established for the future. Here is a moderate democratic Government abolishing an election because it happens to be inconvenient. What will a more malign force do with that one in the years to come?

There is still time for wiser heads to prevail. This is a bad Bill – and Ministers know that very well.

Mail on Sunday, 17.6.84

... AND AFTER IT WAS DEFEATED IN THE LORDS.

WHAT A MESS

The Government had a manifesto mandate to abolish the GLC. It did not have a mandate to make a hash of it. But that is what has happened. Last night's defeat in the Lords was the penalty for the Government's gross and persistent mishandling of the future rule over London.

The plan by Mr Patrick Jenkin, Environment Secretary, to cancel next year's elections for the GLC and the Metropolitan County Councils (with some 13 million voters in all) has now been knocked for six. It is typical of the miscalculation that has dogged this affair that ministers appeared to be taken totally by surprise.

... Ministers would probably do best now to offer to allow the existing GLC members to serve out a few extra months until the full Bill to do away with County Hall becomes law next summer or autumn. Meanwhile, there needs to be a drastic rethink about the hodge podge of boroughs and special boards which the Government has patched together as a substitute for County Hall.

Mr Jenkin has shown no sign that he is ready, able or willing to do that. Come the autumn reshuffle it would be as well for Mrs Thatcher to move this particular Environment Secretary to some other, safer environment.

Standard, 29.6.84

THE LORDS HAVE IT

When the House of Lords votes down a decision of substance by the House of Commons, and does so on grounds of constitutional principle, that is an action which it is right to subject to searching criticism. The Lords' defeat of the government's intention to cancel the elections due to take place next year for the Greater London Council and the Metropolitan Counties, just before these local authorities are due to be abolished, does more than survive such scrutiny. It is plainly an action in the best spirit of the Constitution.

Times, 30.6.84

FUMBLE, BUMBLE & BOTCH

Who would have believed it?

Red Ken Livingstone is now appearing as champion of the British Constitution – courtesy of the Peerage – and a friend of democracy.

That is what the Tories have managed to contrive by their fumbling, bumbling, botched handling of the Bill to abolish the GLC and the other metropolitan councils.

The GLC is a costly excrescence that has provided way-out Lefties with a means of spending public money on their own pet schemes.

Mr Patrick Jenkin, the Environment Secretary, should have had the easiest of jobs demolishing it.

But he has dismally failed.

He has allowed Ken Livingstone to make all the propaganda running, at the ratepayers' expense.

... It is a sad and sorry tale of complacency compounded by incompetence.

What is needed now is a counter-Ken Livingstone publicity campaign conducted with flair and vigour.

On recent evidence this seems to be beyond Mr Jenkin's capacity.

Mrs Thatcher must give the task to someone who can 'mix it' with Red Ken. Someone who will bring fresh ideas to a tired team.

She must get someone of her own mettle to convince the country that we will be far better off without the wasteful, useless GLC and its fellow mega-councils.

Daily Express, 30.6.84

THE CRAZY PAVING BILL

... The humiliation must be all the more galling for the Government since there are any number of Tories, ranging from the party's former national leader to its previous GLC leader, entitled to announce 'We told you so.' Their warnings, however went unheeded and Mrs Thatcher and her Cabinet colleagues have only themselves to thank for the legislative bruise they have now sustained. Not to put too fine a point upon it, their chosen device of doing away with democracy, even in advance of their main local government measure gaining the Royal Assent, smacked from the beginning of sharp constitutional practice.

Observer, 1.7.84

weeks later, at the end of June. The task for the opposition was not merely to get its supporters there but also to devise an amendment which would maximize the chance of all-party support. More inter-party meetings ensued. What emerged was an amendment, tabled with all-party support, being signed by two Labour, one Liberal, one SDP and one Tory peer. The amendment (known as the 'Pym amendment' because a similar one had been tabled by Francis Pym in the Commons) had the effect of ensuring that the elections could not be cancelled until after the main Abolition Bill became law.

This amendment was clearly unacceptable to the government. If carried it would have had the effect of letting the 1985 elections proceed. This was because the main Abolition Bill – which would be both highly complex and long – was not due to be published until November. It could not therefore become law in time to cancel elections due in May.

Faced with this predicament, the government had two options: to proceed and hope to win or to table an alternative amendment less destructive than the Pym amendment. In the event, amid much speculation about likely government tactics, the Cabinet decided to press on. When the opening day of the committee stage arrived on 28 June it was still widely assumed that although the vote would be close, the government would win. In the event, these predictions were wildly wrong. The government suffered, in the words of *The Times*, a 'savage defeat', with the Pym amendment being carried by 191 votes to 143, a huge anti-government majority of 48. Mrs Thatcher's instincts of nine months earlier had been cruelly but belatedly exposed to have been right.

The scale of the defeat astonished most informed observers as well as the opposition whips. It was probably the most damaging defeat of Mrs Thatcher's five years in office. At the time it was felt that the defeat was explained predominantly by the low turnout of Tory peers, who can be whipped to appear once but not twice in such quick succession. Lord Denham, fearful of overkill, had issued only a two-line whip.

In fact, the small vote was explained by abstentions as much as by absenteeism. Analysis of the vote showed that 94 Tory peers who voted for the second reading of the Bill on 11 June

The Lords' defeat of the Paving Bill clause on elections gets a quick response from Ken Livingstone and the County Hall campaigners.

failed to oppose the amendment. Of these, an estimated 40 were in the House on Thursday but chose to abstain. The rest failed to turn up. Although the debate coincided, as cynics pointed out, with the first day of the Lord's Test, the first day of the Henley Regatta and Wimbledon, the real reason for the low turnout appeared to have more to do with a refusal by peers to put themselves out again for a Bill they did not particularly favour.

In contrast to the Tories, the opposition vote held firm, with 114 Labour votes, 40 Alliance, a substantial number of independents and three Tory rebels. With the vote taken at 5.45 p.m., and amidst inevitable scenes of jubilation, opposition celebrations continued through the evening in the Labour whips' office with organizers of the GLC anti-abolition campaign. Within a few days, as if to rub it in further, the sign on the river frontage of County Hall facing Westminster was changed from 'Peers:

Listen to Londoners – Don't scrap the GLC elections' to 'Peers: Thank you for defending London's democracy'.

The despondent Tories did their best to rescue the situation. The charge of hypocrisy against Mr Livingstone, having become leader as the result of a 'Palace Revolution', was repeated. Others pointed to the irony of Labour's victory being dependent on the very body they were keen to abolish. Shrewd observers, however, pointed to the potentially sinister implications of the Lords' decision for a radical and reforming Labour government. If it was prepared to stamp on a Tory government attempting to implement, however ineptly, a manifesto commitment, what damage might it inflict on a future Labour manifesto?

Whatever these side discussions, however, the result was a stunning setback for the government, a body blow to Mrs Thatcher, and by far the most serious of a string of tactical blunders. It was also a bitter personal upset for Mr Jenkin, who was becoming excessively accident-prone. In the Commons the next day there were repeated calls for his resignation.

It also appears that Mr Jenkin did not take his defeat particularly well. On the Friday night, according to *The Sunday Times*, he described to a group of businessmen in Bradford the debate in the Lords: 'One of my colleagues had a party of local constituents from a mental hospital in the public gallery and they watched with growing astonishment – and a growing sense of familiarity.' Among Tory backbenchers, it was Mr Jenkin who was being blamed for the débâcle and was widely tipped as a potential loser in the next reshuffle. Against this it might have been viewed as excessively disloyal for the prime minister to sack a minister for implementing her policies. Mr Jenkin, after all, was little more than a 'messenger boy' for Mrs Thatcher.

Back to square one

After the defeat, a jubilant opposition argued that the elections should now proceed. On the night of the defeat, Ken Livingstone had hailed it as 'an overwhelming victory for democracy. The message to the government could not be clearer. Surely it has now to do the honourable thing – admit its plans are wrong and let next year's GLC elections go ahead.' This, however, was the last thing wanted by the government, even more fearful now of the elections becoming a popular referendum in favour of retention. Mr Jenkin soon made his decision clear not to withdraw the Bill, but to soldier on.

Opposed to letting the elections proceed, he had several options. First he could have tried to reverse any Lords' amendments in the Commons later. This, however, would have risked the Lords and Commons throwing out each other's amendments, further antagonizing the Bill's opponents in both Houses. Such a strategy would also have risked further hostile publicity.

Another option would have been to invoke the Parliament Act. In principle the Lords have only delaying powers. The Commons can insist that a Bill rejected in the Upper House still becomes law, but not for 13 months after the Commons' second reading. Since this would not have been until 12 May 1985, a week after the GLC elections were due, it would have been pointless. This left Mr Jenkin with only one real option, the one rejected at the beginning – to extend the life of the existing GLC and metropolitan counties for one year. This was the course reluctantly adopted – the final irony and a painful somersault which could have been avoided if Mrs Thatcher had stuck by her own instincts and overridden Mr Jenkin.

The essential problem with this strategy, however, remained. By leaving Ken Livingstone and his colleagues in power for another year, it increased the prospect of sabotage. To deal with this, the government had to look for 'Ken-proof' ways of preventing obstruction. On 12 July, at the report stage in the Lords, the government tabled a number of new clauses designed to restrict the opportunities for a spending spree and asset-stripping in the run-up to abolition. They included a ban on the disposal of land without the consent of the Environment Secretary and a requirement for ministerial approval for new contracts for engineering and building works over £250,000 and for all other schemes, including publicity, costing over £100,000. New penalties were introduced involving disqualification from holding office in local government for breach of the legislation.

Together with charges of further authoritarianism, the GLC's response was that such detailed controls would affect over 250 transactions a week and require a deluge of paperwork by the DoE. The GLC claimed that items requiring DoE approval would include choosing the colour of school linoleum, the baked beans bill (the GLC buys in bulk for other boroughs and agencies) and every traffic light scheme. The decision also led to a rush of hurriedly called meetings at County Hall to get projects through before the Paving Bill became law on 26 July. In the two weeks between the announcement of the new regulations and the passing of the Bill, the GLC obtained committee approval for contracts worth £40 million in order to beat the new controls. Subsequently, to reinforce its point, the GLC was to inundate the DoE seeking approval for a good many of its transactions, both important and trivial.

On 24 July, Mr Jenkin also announced his intention to seek powers in the main Abolition Bill requiring the GLC to get ministerial consent for the transfer of resources to the boroughs. In the previous year the GLC had developed a policy of providing assistance to boroughs with particular problems in the form of financial aid to projects such as sports and recreational facilities and voluntary organizations under a new 'stress boroughs programme'. According to the GLC this was aimed at extending the council's redistributive role in favour of the poorer inner-city areas. This policy was, however, frowned upon by the DoE, who believed that the GLC should play only a limited role in redistribution in this way and viewed the policy as a way of shielding Labour councils from the government's new ratecapping measures.

Moreover, because the GLC was planning to expand the programme, and because the Abolition Bill could not become law until the following summer, Mr Jenkin also announced that the new control would apply retrospectively to all transactions as from 24 July – the day of announcement. If cash or assets were disposed of without DoE consent, the boroughs concerned would be required to repay the money together with interest. This put the onus on the boroughs not to cooperate. Mr Jenkin admitted that he found it 'unpalatable' to have to take these powers. Mr Livingstone was quick to condemn the proposal as a 'flagrant and unprecedented abuse of constitutional procedures. This is the arrogance of an elective dictatorship in action'.

In its final form, the Paving Bill was barely recognizable from the original. All that was left in common was the cancellation of the elections. Instead of the proposed interim body the existing council was to continue in power for another eleven months, but in a predominantly subservient role to the DoE, with its new array of centralized powers and controls. None of these controls was contained in the original Bill. They were not inserted at committee stage but during the final report stage when, despite their highly contentious nature, there was least opportunity for adequate debate. Thus was born this highly controversial and centralizing piece of legislation.

Moreover, while the government may have thought it had got its way on the elections, Mr Livingstone had other plans in mind. Not prepared to concede defeat so easily, he and three Labour colleagues resigned their GLC seats on 2 August in order to fight by-elections on the principle of abolition. Mr Jenkin may have avoided a wholesale referendum, but he was not to escape elections entirely.

The by-elections

Mr Livingstone had long been warning Mr Jenkin that if the elections were cancelled he would force by-elections in order to put the government's policy to the test. True to his word, he and his colleagues had now caused four by-elections to be held on 20 September. The aim was to inflict maximum embarrassment on the government, and taunt it to submit itself to the test of the ballot box.

Nevertheless, he was taking a risk. He could have simply resigned his own seat in the knowledge that with his renewed popularity, he would romp home. A Harris poll for 'The London Programme' had forecast that a by-election for his Paddington seat on the principle of abolition would give him a huge majority, with a hefty swing to Labour.

Mr Livingstone decided to forgo such an easy course. Instead, the Labour Group opted for by-elections in Paddington, Hayes and Harlington, Lewisham West and Edmonton. All were

A MESSAGE, BUT NOT A MANDATE

Britain's electoral system lends itself awkwardly to deciding single issues. As an endorsement of the Greater London Council, or rather as a rejection of the government's proposals to 'streamline' it out of existence, Mr Ken Livingstone's by-elections tomorrow are clumsy. A stunt, the Prime Minister called them; so they are, and so is much of politics, local and national. But gamesmanship will not invalidate these contests as a signal of public unease at the restructuring of London's government.

... A turn out tomorrow by voters in Westminster, Hillingdon, Enfield and Lewisham, even in no larger numbers than municipal polls usually attract, ought to occasion misgivings within the Department of the Environment even at this late stage in the preparation of the substantive abolition legislation.

Yet these elections are potentially dangerous. The danger is that a vote registered in protest at the government's plan is seized on by Mr Livingstone and his party as an endorsement of the current controllers of the GLC, as approval of the 'local socialism' practised and preached at County Hall during the past three years, and in evidence in town halls elsewhere in the capital.

... It would be a pity if voters who want to keep the GLC – or some reorganized form of London-wide government became unwitting accomplices of Mr Livingstone's projects for socialist transformation. The polling lists offer, perhaps with the Alliance candidates, alternative expressions.

Times, 19.9.84

THE COST OF KEN

Today Red Ken Livingstone, with three of his Labour comrades, is standing in a by-election.

Does London really want him back?

Consider what he has done as GLC leader.

In nine months, the council has distributed £31 million to voluntary organizations.

Here are just some of the 2,073 groups which have received amounts ranging from £111 to £77, 835.

Babies against the Bomb.
English Collective of Prostitutes.
Irish Women's Group.
Lesbian Line.
Rights of Women (ROW).
Cypriot Community Workers Action Group and Joint

Council for the Welfare of Immigrants.

I Drum.
Migrants Action Group.
London Region CND.
London Region Trade Union Campaign for Nuclear Disarmament.

National Peace Council.
World Disarmament Campaign.
Unity of Afro-Caribbean People.
Southall Black Sisters.
Union of Turkish Workers.
Earth Resource Research.
Hackney Trades Council Trade Union Support Unit.

Hackney Black Women's Association.
Black Amalgamated Self Help Co-op.
Rastafarian Advisory Centre.
Marx Memorial Library.
Chile Democratico GB.
Irish in Islington Project.
Liberation Movement for Colonial Freedom.

Gay Switchboard.
London Lesbian and Gay Centre.
Police Accountability for Community Enlightenment.

Medical Campaign against Nuclear Weapons.

London Women's Liberation Newsletter Collective.

Black Trade Unionist Solidarity Movement.

Abyssinian Society.
Jewish Socialists Group.
See Red Women's Workshop.
Ecumenical unit for Racism Awareness Programme.

Southwark Black Workers Group.
South East London Women for Life on Earth.

Cultural Organization for Black Radical Achievement.

Gay Bereavement Project.
Gay London Police Monitoring Group.

Campaign to Curb Police Powers.
Women's Peace Bus.
Only Women Press.
Spare Rib.

Do you think this is the way ratepayers' money should be spent?

If so, then Red Ken is your man. You deserve him!
Sun, 20.9.84

LEFT IN THE COLD

So now we know. Virtually three out of four Londoners cannot be bothered to turn out to vote to save the Greater London Council. Despite the expert and expensive Labour publicity campaign, despite the Government's failure to mount any sort of convincing campaign, the great abolition row leaves most people cold.

... Had Ken Livingstone's fantasy been fact, the populace would have swarmed out, rain or shine, to save the GLC they love and give its leader a resounding vote of confidence he sought. It didn't happen.

Standard, 21.9.84

A VOTE FOR – WHAT?

If the Prime Minister is finished with the Greater London Council, so also is Mr Ken Livingstone. The expensive little rhapsody of Mr Livingstone's time in local government was given a final fling with Thursday's by-elections. The GLC can now be safely abolished and Mr Livingstone can go on to the constituency of his choice and a brilliant career in national politics ... He is a major politician and Labour can now start getting worried or excited about him. He is more astute than Mr Benn, better able to simulate likeableness while remaining quite outstandingly ruthless with anyone innocently getting in his way, something to which Mr Reg Freeson can testify.

Daily Telegraph, 22.9.84

marginal seats, with Labour GLC members but Conservative MPs (though boundary changes between the GLC and general elections had slightly altered the profiles of the seats). The Group intended to make it difficult for the Tories to refuse to participate.

The by-elections caused considerable wrangling within the London Conservative Party. The Party chairman, John Selwyn Gummer, immediately denounced them as a gimmick and the kind of Labour stunt the government hoped to end by the abolition of the GLC. But this view was far from universally shared within the local Conservative Associations. While some echoed it, others wanted to seize the opportunity of ending Ken Livingstone's control of County Hall. Other Tories argued that not to stand would disenfranchise Conservative voters, give the SDP a free run, and sacrifice the opportunity of publicizing how Mr Livingstone was running the GLC. In Paddington, in defiance of Central Office instructions, several wards voted to field a candidate. In the end the powerful hand of Central Office had its way. Labour's challenge was refused. The Tories boycotted all four by-elections.

At a press conference on the day of his resignation, Mr Livingstone read out a statement from the Labour leader, Neil Kinnock, announcing the 'full and committed support of the whole Labour Party'. It did not go unnoticed that this was in stark contrast to the position 18 months earlier, when Ken

Livingstone was seen as a total embarrassment to the Labour leadership in the run-up to the general election. From the outset, the SDP–Liberal Alliance made it clear that they would be contesting the elections, also on an anti-abolition platform; the GLC Alliance Group leader, Liberal Adrian Slade, dubbed the prospective Tory boycott 'lily-livered'.

As the closing date for candidate nominations drew near, despite the lack of official Tory candidates, there was still widespread speculation about who would stand. At one stage Sir Alfred Sherman, co-founder of the right-wing Centre for Policy Studies, was invited by rebel Paddington Conservatives to stand unofficially but declined. In one constituency, West Lewisham, Michael Moore, Chairman of the East Lewisham Young Conservatives, fought as the 'Pro-Abolition Alliance' candidate.

As the election campaign got under way, unofficial Tory candidates appeared in two constituencies – Hayes and Harlington and Edmonton. Both were accused of being stooge candidates by local Tory leaders, who declared they were not known to the local association. One was a member of CND and the other had CND and peace stickers in the front door of her council flat. Tories alleged that they were Labour supporters masquerading as Tories. Later, both claimed they were not Tories, nor Labour stooges, but were standing in order to give Tories someone to vote for and had not been put up to it. Both subsequently withdrew.

Halfway through the campaign a leading GLC Tory councillor and former contender for the GLC Tory leadership, George Tremlett, urged Tories to vote Labour in the by-elections. In the late 1970s, he had become a figure hated by Labour because of his housing policies when he was GLC chairman of housing. Gradually, however, he had become disillusioned with his own party's policies and the effect cuts in public spending were having on inner-city stress. Standing side-by-side with Ken Livingstone at a press conference during the campaign, George Tremlett urged that as the elections were being fought

on a fundamental issue of principle, of whether London should have its own elected government, my message to voters is to support Ken – not Ken *per se*, but for the principle on which he is standing.

Following repeated calls for his sacking from the GLC Conservative Group, Mr Tremlett wrote an article in the *Standard* (10 September) in which he claimed that the real reason for Mrs Thatcher's decision to abolish the GLC was that having 'dealt with enemies abroad [the Falklands] she was now going to deal with enemies at home [Ken Livingstone and Arthur Scargill]'. Subsequently George Tremlett was dropped from the GLC Conservative Group.

The by-elections were potentially of very great significance for both Ken Livingstone and the government. If Labour had won the elections on a reasonable turnout, they would have demonstrated considerable public unease about abolition. If Labour had lost even one of the elections, Ken Livingstone's strategy would have disastrously backfired. In the event the results were indecisive as a measure of the strength of public opinion. Labour was returned with large majorities in each of the four seats, although their vote fell compared with 1981 in three of them. In Paddington, Mr Livingstone received 78 per cent of the vote and increased his majority dramatically. The results were poor for the SDP–Liberal Alliance, who averaged only 23 per cent of the vote in the four constituencies despite the absence of Tory candidates and a hard-fought campaign.

Labour inevitably heralded the results as a major victory, and Mr Livingstone immediately pointed out that a majority of Conservative MPs in London were now at risk. The low turnouts, however, from a high of 29.6 per cent in Paddington to a low of 20 per cent in Edmonton – even allowing for continuous torrential rain on the day and the Tory boycott – were a major disappointment to Labour, and completely undermined their strategy. Having declared at the start that a 40 per cent poll was needed to justify the elections, Livingstone's victory claim sounded pretty hollow.

6. IS THE GLC REDUNDANT?

I do not believe you need two tiers of local government, and I very much regret that Horace Cutler has not been the ruthless Tory he likes to project and come forward with the biggest axe of all and axed the whole appalling show. (Ken Livingstone, GLC debate on the Marshall Report, March 1979)

All through the debates on the Paving Bill, the Thatcher government was frequently accused of not having thought things through, of having rushed into the whole business. This impression had been strongly reinforced by the publication of *Streamlining the Cities*, the White Paper setting out the details of the government's plan in October 1983. This 'pathetic document' – as Jim Sharpe, an Oxford don and expert in local government affairs, had described it – purported to explain what was wrong with the GLC and to outline the new arrangements that would replace it in just 32 pages. One section, headed 'The Case for Change', occupied only ten short paragraphs.

Inevitably academics like Jim Sharpe contrasted the flimsy White Paper with the Report of the Herbert Commission in 1960 which had led to the GLC being set up. That report had run to hundreds of pages and had taken three years to prepare. In this light many people found it difficult to take *Streamlining the Cities* seriously; it seemed to confirm the view that the motive behind the attack on the GLC was almost entirely party political, to rid Mrs Thatcher of a troublesome political foe. But, as we have seen, calls for the abolition of the GLC had already been made by politicians on all sides at the end of the 1970s including, on one memorable occasion, Ken Livingstone himself.

Party politicians can, of course, be notoriously fickle, their opinions being coloured by whether they are in power or in opposition, and London politicians are no exception. Nevertheless, support for the abolition of the GLC does seem, for a time at least, to have run across the party divide. It reflected a broad degree of unanimity that the GLC had failed to do the job it was set up to do and had become increasingly irrelevant to Londoners' needs.

The GLC planning fiasco

To grasp fully the extent to which the GLC had failed to live up to the expectations of its creators we have to remind ourselves of the conclusions of the Herbert Report of 1960.

Herbert had accepted that the new London boroughs have to be the 'primary' units of local government in the capital.

However, the report argued that there were certain 'all-London' functions that could not be handled by the boroughs on their own. Most of all there seemed to be a clear need for an all-London council to plan and coordinate the future development of the capital. Planning was to be taken out of the hands of civil servants in Whitehall and placed under local democratic control. Planning, in this sense, was not conceived of as a passive process of drawing up maps of existing London and tacking on new areas of development. (Such areas were, in any case, severely restricted by the Green Belt policy.) Planning was to be an active affair, seeking to mould the whole of Greater London into a coherent whole. The location of new factories or offices was to be planned to minimize environmental damage and ensure that it took place where it was needed, not just where it wanted to go. A new road system would be planned to relieve the problems of chronic traffic congestion and at the same time bring real economic benefit to trade and commerce. The needs of public transport were to be considered too. Working at the centre, the new Greater London Council was to be the architect of a new and better capital through the Greater London Development Plan (the GLDP).

If this was the new GLC's greatest challenge, it was only too soon to emerge as arguably its greatest failure. The council was to fall at its very first hurdle. To some extent this was due to a lack of experience, inevitable perhaps at this bold new frontier of local government work. But the planners were also to display a less forgivable lack of vision.

The task itself was daunting enough. It involved collating information on London as it then existed, assessing likely future trends in its population and its level of economic activity and making value judgements on such matters as where to encourage new commercial and industrial development and where to try and stop it. The planning team at County Hall took about four years to draw up its new blueprint for the capital before unveiling it to the world in March 1969.

The time taken to prepare the GLDP had only served to heighten the expectations of those who looked to the GLC to show what advantages could spring from an all-London planning system under local democratic control. Just before the publication of the new plan Peter Hall, an academic who had done much to popularize the idea of planning, could barely restrain his enthusiasm. The GLDP, he wrote, 'is rumoured to be a powerful and imaginative document...' But only a few weeks later, on publication of the draft plan, he was forced into a hasty reappraisal. 'The statement [he now glumly concluded] is flat, unimaginative, unoriginal, unmemorable.'

Mr Hall was not alone in roundly condemning this first product of the new planning machinery at County Hall. The draft GLDP was, frankly, a disappointing document. And its real shortcomings were to be embarrassingly exposed in the public inquiry that sat to consider objections (28,000 in all) to the GLDP proposals.

The 'Panel of Inquiry', headed by Sir Frank Layfield, a leading planning lawyer, sat for more than half a year and subjected the GLC planners to a withering cross-examination. In the end it issued a report damning much of the draft plan as unrealistic and excessively vague. It observed that many of the policies were expressed in such a way that they 'could mean anything to anyone'. Its points of criticism were so numerous and its comments so detailed that in effect the Layfield Report, rather than the GLC draft, formed the basis of the Greater London Plan.

The whole affair seemed to throw into question the ability of the GLC to live up to its role as the metropolitan planning authority. It also imposed a long period of delay on the whole planning process. Layfield reported in 1972 and there then followed long and detailed consultation between the Department of the Environment in Whitehall and the GLC. The final draft of the GLDP was not given formal approval by the council until 1976.

The delay further weakened the GLC. By this time much of the statistical basis of the plan was out of date, making appeals against it more likely to succeed. On top of this the London boroughs, who actually dealt at first hand with all planning applications, had developed a strong sense of their own independence. Having done without a GLDP for eleven years, they were now much less inclined to fall in with its all-London planning approach. Surprisingly, perhaps, the Department of the Environment itself, asked to adjudicate where planning disputes arose between the councils, usually came out against the GLC.

The late arrival of the GLDP was a setback from which the GLC was never to recover but, in retrospect, it is clear that the odds had been stacked very heavily against the County Hall planners from the start. They found themselves lacking any real power, sandwiched between strong borough authorities on the one hand, and on the other a central government unwilling to surrender a final say in how the capital should develop.

Even before 1976 central government had intervened to stop the GLC plan to demolish the Covent Garden district. Since then – in 1979 – the GLC has lost what control it had over the redevelopment of London Docklands. That responsibility was handed to the London Docklands Development Corporation, an *ad hoc* government creation. Even more recently Environment Secretaries have intervened to take personal responsibility for the future of central London sites such as that at Vauxhall Cross and Hay's Wharf. Both these look on to the River Thames and should have been jewels in the GLC crown, akin to the South Bank site, planned and developed by the old LCC.

Faced with its record of 20 years of failure or irrelevance it is tempting to ask, in the case of planning at least, who needs the GLC?

Thwarted in the suburbs

But, of course, the GLC exists for more than simply planning for London. Had its record been better elsewhere, its lack of success in shaping the present-day face of the capital could easily be forgiven. However, it is hard to avoid the conclusion that in other quite crucial areas of County Hall responsibility the GLC has been little more successful.

When the GLC took over as the all-London council in 1965 there was one pressing all-London problem that it seemed admirably qualified to deal with, the terrible shortage of housing. Only a month before its first formal meeting, a government report had focused public attention on the large number of

Londoners who lived in substandard private rented accommodation, mostly in the Victorian inner core of the capital. The Milner Holland Committee documented as never before the huge scale of the problem. It found that half a million families (over $1\frac{1}{2}$ million people) had no access to the basic amenity of a bath. A quarter of a million families were judged to be overcrowded. But, most interesting of all, the problem was heavily concentrated in a few London boroughs. Islington was the worst. In some areas population density was as high as 300 to the acre. Milner Holland reckoned that to bring housing standards up to an acceptable level 30 per cent, or nearly one in three of the population of the borough, would have to be rehoused outside its boundaries. Other boroughs, such as Hackney, were not much better placed. In the view of the committee, here was a challenge to be met on a capital-wide basis:

land will be needed in the outer areas and outside London to receive persons displaced from the inner areas. If the attack on shortages and bad housing conditions is to be successful, it must be planned, applied and directed for London as a whole.

This was a challenge to which the new GLC was anxious to rise. It had inherited the old LCC housing department with a stock of some 236,000 homes (mainly concentrated in inner London) and, more importantly, some 8,000 construction workers and a large on-going building programme. But the County Hall planners soon found there was a major snag. Following the recommendations of the Herbert Commission, the Macmillan government had made the London boroughs the chief housing authorities across the capital; under the London Government Act they were eventually to take over the GLC housing stock and it was assumed, in the meantime, that they would take charge of building in their own areas.

The Act had presumed, however, that the GLC would step in to tackle housing problems which were clearly beyond the resources or capabilities of a single borough. The GLC was empowered to draw up plans for an all-London housing strategy and was expected, with the resources it had at its disposal, to supplement any effort made by the boroughs. In the light of

Milner Holland this now emerged as a much more important role than those drafting the Act had anticipated.

It was one thing for the Act to define the GLC's role in relation to housing, it was quite another when the council tried to put theory into practice. For the Act made it clear that the GLC could step in only with the consent of the boroughs concerned or with specific ministerial sanction. This soon emerged as a fatal qualification of County Hall's power.

The first chair of the GLC Housing Committee was Evelyn (now Lady) Denington, a former LCC member who assumed that the new council would work like the old county council writ large. One of her first official visits in her new capacity was to Islington, where the scale of the housing problem galvanized her into action. She became quite convinced that the new outer London suburbs (where population densities were as low as 20 to the acre) would just have to agree to allow the GLC to build there to relieve the pressure.

But her next step, at Bromley Borough Council, dispelled any illusions she had that the new 'Greater London' had any sense of being 'one city', ready to share the common burdens of the capital. In 1984 she could still recall vividly the shock she experienced at the hands of the Bromley Council: 'There was no understanding at all, one felt there wasn't a desire to understand, it was an "I'm-all-right Jack" attitude, you know, "Leave me alone ... count me out".'

It was clear from the start that the outer suburbs, for the most part, dreaded the idea of hordes of displaced inner-London council tenants coming to live among them, partly because they might 'bring down the tone' of an area, partly because they were likely to be Labour voters who could swing the political balance on the councils. The real question, then, was whether the GLC had the necessary power to override their opposition. The experience of Evelyn Denington seemed to confirm that the provisions of the Act in this respect were largely a dead letter.

Despite the unhelpful attitude of Bromley, Lady Denington endeavoured to press ahead with a programme in the old LCC style but she soon found that, without the cooperation of the boroughs, the task was beyond the capacity of the GLC. Planning the new housing programme depended crucially on finding suitable sites and, in the sprawling suburbs of outer London, this was no easy task. Without the cooperation of the boroughs, who as planning authorities held the vital information, it proved to be almost impossible. Faced with a general refusal on the part of the boroughs to produce details of where land was available, Evelyn Denington virtually gave up the attempt to establish a GLC building programme in the suburbs. Sometimes rebel Labour councillors in the outer boroughs, such as Merton, leaked information to the GLC but as a rule the GLC considered it too sensitive an issue to act upon. (There were some exceptions to the general picture, such as the Barnet Airfield site in North London where the local council allowed the GLC to build an estate.)

In the end Evelyn Denington settled for a much less controversial policy of allowing boroughs to build for themselves on condition that the GLC had the right to 'nominate' some tenants from its own housing list, but this policy delivered few places for GLC tenants. It also had the effect of further undermining the GLC role in the future since, in return for nomination rights, the GLC had often to promise never to build properties of its own in the borough concerned. The attempt by the GLC to implement a housing strategy received a further setback when the Tories won the GLC elections of 1967. Horace Cutler, the new housing chairman, came from outer London and virtually brought the policy to a halt.

In the 1970s attempts were again made to resuscitate a County Hall housing role in response to further damning housing reports but, even with the active support of the Heath government, a Tory GLC committed to a big building programme ran into similar blocking tactics on the part of the suburbs. Then the Labour government of 1974 combined with a Labour-controlled GLC in a last-ditch effort. The GLC Labour manifesto of 1973 had talked optimistically of building homes for a million people and of seeking 'new powers' to sweep aside suburban obstruction. But nothing really came of it. Economic storm clouds gathered ominously after the oil crisis of 1973 and neither the British government nor the GLC could isolate themselves from the prevailing climate. When Anthony Crosland announced 'the party's over' in May 1975 the axe fell as heavily on council spending in London as anywhere else. The socialist vision of the 1973 manifesto largely evaporated in its aftermath.

The curtain was brought down on the tragi-comedy of the GLC housing strategy by the new Tory-dominated council elected in 1977. Horace Cutler, the new leader of the GLC, pushed ahead with a policy of transferring the GLC stock of houses and flats to the boroughs as envisaged by the Act of 1963. Those reluctant to take on the aging GLC tenements or its new 'industrialized-built' estates in inner London were eventually forced to give way by the Thatcher government returned to Westminster in 1979.

This could be said to have brought County Hall ambitions to make a significant impact on the capital's housing problems to a final end. The history of 1965 to 1980 shows that the GLC's dream of opening up the suburbs to poorly housed inner-city families was thwarted by a combination of changing political control and lack of power to force its strategy on the uncooperative outer boroughs. The GLC found its housing role largely confined to building in inner London with borough consent.

Since 1980 the GLC has attempted to develop a new role in housing. This has included help for the single homeless and a programme for improving the old GLC homes now in borough hands. But this work itself has been greatly restricted by central government control over capital spending on housing.

The loss of the GLC's major housing functions was to throw a further question mark over the future of County Hall. The *Observer*, in an article written in 1975 when the new GLC 'Strategic Housing Plan' looked like failing, had commented pointedly that '... regional housing strategy is the GLC's claim to salvation. If it fails in that, what is it there for?'

Going off the rails

In 1975 one answer might have been – 'to run London Transport'. In the eyes of the electors this was the most up-front responsibility of County Hall. More informed observers might have added 'to plan and build London's major roads'. Taken together, these two functions, grouped broadly under the GLC

'Department of Transport and Transportation', still remained of vital importance to London's well-being. But even here critics of the GLC can point to glaring shortcomings in the post-1965 arrangements for governing the capital city. No matter how talented and dedicated the leadership at County Hall might have been (and it was often none too inspired) the GLC was up against it from the start.

In the first place, the council of 1965 had transport responsibilities without actually controlling London's public transport system. The tubes and buses were run by one nationalized operator, London Transport, and the commuter railway network by another, the British Railways Board. It was, perhaps, only natural in these circumstances for the new council to look to those matters where it had direct control, the planning and building of London's main roads.

The outcome was the production of the abortive plan of 1969 to build a huge urban motorway network as recommended by the Abercrombie Report of 1944. Costing billions of pounds, it would have given the capital a series of four 'ringways' on a scale worthy of Los Angeles. The GLC plan ran into trouble from the start as it coincided with a new wave of opposition to obtrusive urban highways that could be built only by destroying good residential property. Of the 28,000 objections to the Layfield Panel of Inquiry, 24,000 were to the motorway proposals.

In the end none of the urban motorways was to be built, although 'Ringway Four' survives as the M25. Layfield came out in favour of 'Ringway One' – the so-called 'Motorway Box' – but the Labour victory in the 1973 GLC elections brought it to power pledged to scrap the plan. Eight years of painstaking work by the County Hall planners was thus written off and new road-building came virtually to a halt amid the loud complaints of the Roads Lobby.

But by this time attention was being switched to public transport as offering an alternative solution to London's traffic problem. In 1969 the London Transport Act had handed the tube and 'red bus' services over to the control of the elected councillors of the GLC. Surprisingly, the London Transport board was allowed to continue for some time operating at 'arm's length' from its new political masters. The new Labour GLC of 1973 was determined to put a stop to that and was committed first to a 'fares freeze' and ultimately to the introduction of free travel (paid for out of the rates). In the economic turmoil of the mid-seventies the Labour Group lost its nerve and the plan to revolutionize London Transport came to nothing. But in opposition after 1977 a new strategy was carefully thought out to put an end to the continuing decline in passengers carried. The result was the celebrated 'Fares Fair' policy of 1981 that brought the new Labour leader, Ken Livingstone, into headlong collision with Bromley Council.

The subsequent House of Lords ruling that this policy was 'unlawful' was a bitter blow to the GLC's authority but, arguably more important, it opened up a debate on the whole future of public transport in London and laid bare the functional short-comings of the existing arrangements. Bromley's Conservative council were sworn foes of Ken Livingstone's brand of left-wing socialism but, as we have seen, they also considered it was unjust to expect Bromley ratepayers to subsidize tube services that were concentrated largely north of the Thames and which they seldom used. The anomaly of GLC control of London Transport but British Rail control of commuter railways, especially important in south London, was there for all to see.

As it happened, the House of Commons Select Committee on Transport was already looking in detail at the capital, in terms of both roads and public transport. The committee, an all-party body, had been taking evidence for two years and, in July 1982, published its conclusions. It found that the main road system in London was in a 'scandalous state' and argued that these roads were of national importance. In order to see some improvement it recommended that the GLC should be stripped of its responsibilities as a highways authority. In its place there should be a new 'Metropolitan Transport Authority' that would cover a wider area than the GLC in order to permit better coordination of roads policy.

The committee linked this with a critique of the existing arrangements for public transport in the capital, pointing out the awkward split between London Transport and British Rail and the fact that the present GLC boundaries did not coincide with either local transport network. The committee concluded that both London Transport services and those of the British Rail commuter lines should be controlled by the same new Metropolitan Transport Authority.

As a gesture to the GLC the committee recommended that it should be allowed to nominate members of the proposed Metropolitan Transport Authority – but it would share the 50 per cent of the authority membership allocated to the local authorities with the surrounding Home Counties and the London boroughs.

In the minds of some London Conservative MPs, like John Wheeler, the Select Committee Report amounted to 'the last nail in the coffin of the GLC'. It was, indeed, potent ammunition for the 'Abolish the GLC' lobby. But it also proved useful in another way: it provided a quasi-justification for the London Regional Transport Act of 1984 that removed all GLC responsibility for the running of one of its last remaining London-wide services. People like John Wheeler could argue that the GLC had now very little to do and could no longer justify its existence.

Unforeseen difficulties

On the surface, then, there seemed to be a good case for the abolition of the Greater London Council when, in May 1983, Mrs Thatcher insisted on inserting her pledge into the Tory manifesto. The GLC had not fulfilled the hopes of the sixties that it would create a solid planning framework for London. It had not made its mark as a strategic housing authority and had lost its housing management role more or less entirely. It had not proved to be an ideal mechanism for the coordination and control of London's public transport services. In fact, to many Tories, the GLC had become a large and bureaucratic monster desperately looking for a role to play that might justify its existence. Under Ken Livingstone it seemed to be assuming more and more the form of a highly political beast, less interested in traditional local government concerns than in adopting postures on national and even international issues. That, in their eyes, was a true indication of the bankruptcy of County Hall as an institution.

The apparent clarity of the case, based on broad political judgement rather than on detailed analysis, may have led Mrs Thatcher and her closest supporters into thinking that abolition would be an easy reform to put into practice. The Conservative manifesto certainly made it seem so, devoting a mere nine lines to the abolition of both the GLC and the metropolitan county councils and referring inaccurately to 'returning' powers to the boroughs that they had in fact never possessed. That manifesto acknowledged that there would be some functions that the boroughs would not be able to manage on their own, but it blandly assumed that these would be run by joint boards of borough councillors, creating a simple and comprehensible new local government structure for London.

When Mrs Thatcher was safely back in Number 10 after the June election her new Secretary of State for the Environment, Patrick Jenkin, announced that a White Paper, spelling out the details of the government's proposals, would be ready by the autumn. Only afterwards did the enormity of the task facing the civil servants really sink in. Their discomfiture began to emerge, often by means of Whitehall leaks that found their way into the national press.

In the first place this proposed reform of London government was, in essence, quite different from any previous reform. In the past there had always been a single successor body to take over the administrative machinery of the body being replaced. In 1965 the GLC had taken over the central bureaucracy from the London County Council; it had also taken on its debts, its records and its stock of property. Now, under the Thatcher scheme, the GLC was to be broken up and, in theory at least, divided out among the existing 32 London boroughs. This was bound to create a severe administrative headache, especially since the GLC political leadership had banned the council officials from cooperating with Whitehall in any way.

Some of the problems inherent in abandoning London-wide local government after nearly a century of existence were so complex that the civil servants could suggest only one way of doing it. New all-London bodies would have to be created to deal with specific areas of difficulty. One of these was the GLC pension fund, which would need continued management even after the GLC had gone, especially since it had become a fund not just for GLC employees and ex-employees but for many other concerns that had been allowed to join it because they had no pension fund of their own. Eventually the civil servants proposed a special GLC Residuary Body to carry on the work after abolition.

This sort of unforeseen complexity was only one reason for the civil servants' unease. Another was the huge range of activities carried out by County Hall, many in themselves of no great political importance, for which provision would still have to be made.* The GLC has responsibility for a ragbag of minor services and duties that include running coroners' courts, providing building inspectors for the whole of inner London, licensing places of entertainment and ensuring the safety of London's reservoirs, as well as for more substantial responsibilities such as disposing of the capital's annual three and a half million tons of household rubbish and running the fire service.

At the Marsham Street headquarters of the DoE these functions had to be broken down into those that could be done by individual boroughs and those that could not. Those in the latter category proved to be more common than the supporters of abolishing the GLC had perhaps anticipated. The list eventually included not just the obvious candidates such as education, the fire service and London-wide planning, but others where County Hall's involvement was less well publicized. Hampstead Heath, for all its apparent informality, was a GLC park that ran across three borough boundaries. The GLC was responsible for the capital's civil defence planning and for dealing with emergencies such as the Moorgate tube disaster. The traffic in London's streets was kept on the move only by a computer-controlled traffic lights system run from County Hall. And, despite the loss of its housing management role, the GLC still ran a huge maintenance and housing improvement programme on behalf of the boroughs.

* Before abolition became a fiercely contested political issue even the London Fire Brigade was run in a way that concealed the GLC's controlling role. When Mrs Thatcher announced her plan to wind up County Hall, the letters G.L.C. were quickly placed on the side of every fire engine.

JOINT BOARDS, COMMITTEES AND QUANGOS

A 'joint board' is usually a single function local authority (set up by statute) which provides a service across a number of boroughs. It is run not by a directly elected council but by a 'board' made up of 1 or more councillors from each of the boroughs. The 'board' determines policy by means of the simple majority vote of its member councillors. The cost of running the service is paid for by raising a rate (or precept) across all its constituent boroughs.

A 'voluntary joint committee' is a non-statutory association of representatives from more than one borough. It has no power to enforce its decision by means of a majority vote so agreement to any joint policy has to be unanimous. Any costs incurred are allocated to the participating boroughs by agreement.

A 'quango' (short for 'quasi-autonomous non-governmental organization') is a non-elected body, such as the Arts Council. Its members are appointed by the government and it is responsible to a government minister (not to parliament). In some cases 'quangos' have the power to raise precept, for instance in the case of the Thames Water Authority.

Before the curtains were brought down at County Hall some alternative machinery for running all these services would have to be found. Over the summer of 1983 this was the problem that was to tax the ingenuity and patience of the Marsham Street bureaucracy given the job of preparing the White Paper for its October deadline. As the drafting proceeded the simple structure proposed in the Conservative manifesto – with the boroughs taking on most of the GLC's tasks and the rest going to a few 'joint boards' – seemed increasingly unachievable. Leaks to the press hinted darkly that numerous special bodies – 'joint boards' and 'quangos' – would be needed to fill the vacuum created by the loss of County Hall.

It came as something of a relief, therefore, when Patrick Jenkin announced at the press conference held to unveil the White Paper – controversially entitled *Streamlining the Cities* – that, for London, there would be only two joint boards with the possibility of a third, and a single new quango – the London Planning Commission. All the other cross-borough issues would be dealt with by already existing bodies or by 'voluntary co-operation' between boroughs.

Across at County Hall the reaction to the White Paper was nevertheless predictably hostile and swift. Ken Livingstone dismissed it as a 'pig's breakfast'. The GLC Tory Group, which has opposed the Thatcher scheme from the start, was scarcely less scathing. Its leader, Alan Greengross, described the plan as 'a ratepayer's nightmare and a bureaucrat's dream'.

The condemnation echoing across the Thames from County Hall was based not so much on what Patrick Jenkin had said as on a quick perusal of the White Paper itself. The government's proposals were, on closer examination, not so clear-cut as the Secretary of State had implied. There proved to be another two new quangos tucked away in the small print of *Streamlining the Cities* (London Regional Transport and the Residuary Body) as well as new involvement in London affairs for at least three others (the Thames Water Authority, the Arts Council and the Royal Commission on Historical Monuments) with the possibility of a fourth (the Sports Council).

To add further to the complexity of the plan to replace the GLC it emerged over the following weeks, through the issue of more detailed 'consultation documents', that the government anticipated the need for 'voluntary joint committees' for such areas as traffic management and parklands. What was more, it was recognized that these arrangements might not work and that some direct central government involvement would be necessary to make sure that they did. In the specific cases of the joint boards for education and fire, the government declared its intention to control both the budget and the manpower levels for the first three years, drawing it into detailed control of day-to-day activities.

The White Paper left many threads untied, but there was to be a period of consultation lasting nearly four months. At the end of that time the government had received 2,300 submissions, many from organizations hostile to the whole idea of abolition, but others from interested parties more concerned about the impact of the plan on their own little patch.

Two Kens square up. Kenneth Baker and Ken Livingstone prepare
to debate the abolition of the GLC in the LWT special programme,
'The Battle for London', October 1984.

The opinion polls of the summer of 1984 showed the GLC was
winning the propaganda battle.

In the light of these representations the government made no real concessions to the underlying principles of its abolition scheme. But it did agree to make one major change. This was in relation to the Inner London Education Authority. Under the original proposals the ILEA was to become a 'joint board' and would have had a virtually built-in Labour majority, since the inner-London borough councils were heavily socialist in composition. First Sir Keith Joseph, the Education Secretary, and then the whole Cabinet were won over by the argument, strongly pressed by David Smith, the Tory minority leader on the ILEA, that the board for inner London education should be directly elected. Thus the old 'School Board of London', absorbed by the LCC in 1904 when single-purpose authorities were going out of fashion, was to be surprisingly resurrected.

The consultation process yielded other less dramatic changes. The replies flooding into the Department of the Environment highlighted the grave concern among many voluntary organizations that their operations could be severely damaged by the loss of their GLC grants (see pp. 132–3). The DoE also accepted that its proposals for a new borough town planning structure was over-complicated, and now opted for what it considered to be a better approach. Even so, the fact that yet more consultation documents on planning were being issued as late as July 1984 gave some indication of the difficulties faced by civil servants unable to get cooperation from the GLC yet under pressure to meet a November deadline.

As this frantic behind-the-scenes activity went on, the government was being placed very much on the defensive by the defeat of the central Paving Bill proposal in the House of Lords. The discomfiture was added to by the enormously successful propaganda war waged by the Livingstone GLC and the inept performance of Patrick Jenkin in the Commons. Over the summer Mrs Thatcher clearly decided that the rot had to stop. She might have considered moving Mr Jenkin to a less exposed position in the government, but he was too closely identified with the abolition plan to make that a practical move in political terms. Instead she brought in as his second-in-command a bright and smooth-talking ex-London MP – Kenneth Baker –

who had been a public relations success in promoting the glossy hi-tech attractions of Information Technology.

Kenneth Baker, whatever his personal feelings about the move, appeared ready to rise to the challenge despite an obvious flaw in his armoury. In 1977 he had been the co-author of a pamphlet calling for a stronger GLC and less central interference in local government. Like so many of the politicians destined to debate the question of London government across the years (including both Patrick Jenkin and Ken Livingstone), he was now apparently required to stand on his political head. He was appointed a few days before the results of the GLC by-elections – something of a damp squib for Ken Livingstone – were announced, and he handled the results with some skill. He was able to follow this with two effective television debates in which he showed that, contrary to all appearances up until then, the GLC leader did not have a monopoly of the arguments.

The fact that the leading combatants were more evenly matched did little to relieve the unease of the battle-scarred ranks of the DoE bureaucracy. When the Abolition Bill was published the debate was bound to revolve around the key issues of efficiency and value for money on the one hand and local democracy on the other. The prospect of an enthralling parliamentary struggle was opening up as MPs and peers looked at the Bill – finally published in November – in the detail it deserved.

7. 'A GHASTLY MESS'?

I do not believe that the arrangements in the Bill as it stands can be said by the government to be either more democratic or more effective, or more likely to be more efficient and less costly. The onus is on the government. (Geoffrey Rippon, former Environment Secretary, speaking in the House of Commons, 4 December 1984)

The publication of the Local Government Bill in November 1984 marked a new phase in the political battle over the future government of the capital. It ran to some 98 clauses and 17 schedules but even then it left unresolved some of the more troublesome details, such as the future of the last big GLC housing development at Thamesmead. Nevertheless, it was now possible for MPs to begin a detailed scrutiny of the Thatcher/Jenkin vision of what the new London would be like. They could attempt to assess just how successful the civil servants had been in their mammoth task of replacing what was generally accepted as an ineffectual GLC/borough system with something better.

When the debate on the second reading began on 3 December the battle lines were already being drawn. The measure was going to be judged largely by the twin standards of how efficient the new arrangements would be and by how far democratic control would be undermined or enhanced.

A more efficient London?

In the debate MPs largely saw 'efficiency' in straightforward bread-and-butter terms – would ratepayers find a somewhat lighter rate bill dropping through their letter boxes or would the costs of running London's local government actually go up? In the opinion of one critic, ex-Prime Minister Edward Heath, no proper answer could be given to this question because there had not been 'an independent and impartial inquiry'. He clearly thought that if there had been the government might have avoided finding itself in 'a ghastly mess'. None the less, it was now possible to look at the overall 'efficiency' and 'cost-effective' arguments in more detail than ever before.

The main plank of the government's case on efficiency had always been, in the words of the manifesto, that the GLC was 'wasteful and unnecessary'. At the outset Patrick Jenkin had hazarded an estimate that savings in a single year as a result of abolition of both the GLC and the metropolitan county councils could be as high as £120 million, but this figure had been withdrawn from circulation on the advice of his more knowledgeable civil servants. Now, just before the second reading debate, his new deputy, Kenneth Baker, had produced the first hard figures to back the government's claim that rate-payers would be better off. Mr Baker divided his savings estimates under two heads: money that would be saved from more efficient operation – so-called 'rationalization savings' – and money saved through less extravagant spending policies – 'policy savings'.

The new Minister for Local Government argued, as expected, that the present GLC/borough framework for governing London was inherently inefficient because, in some ares, the two tiers duplicated each other's work. As this duplication was to be eliminated there would be 'scope for substantial savings'. Mr Baker put the figure not far below the level that Mr Jenkin had originally hoped for – an estimated saving of some £50 million for the GLC alone. This would, however, not be achieved in the first year after abolition because of compensation that would have to be paid to those who lost their jobs. This figure could be as high as £20 million.

At County Hall the figures were treated with a degree of incredulity. A week earlier the GLC accountants had produced their own estimate of the financial consequences of abolition. The press release boldly announced – with a hint of understatement – 'GLC ABOLITION WILL COST £225 MILLION – AT LEAST'.

Reading through the small print, however, it emerged that this figure referred to a five-year period. MPs trying to establish some common ground between the wildly differing forecasts could light upon the estimates for redundancy pay – both sides agreeing on the figure of £20 million. This at least implied a common acceptance that some of the present County Hall workforce would not be able to find re-employment within a local government framework. But there was otherwise irritatingly little on which the two assessments could be compared and put to the test.

The government, anxious not to offer any hostages to fortune, risked being specific about savings in only two areas. One of these was to be in axing the GLC Planning Department. Under the present arrangements this is one source of undeniable duplication. Planning law requires that anyone wishing to put up a new building, substantially extend an existing one or change the use of it, has to submit a planning application to the local planning authority, in the case of London the local borough council. If the proposal is for a new 'superstore', to take one example, the plans will first be scrutinized by the borough planners, who will also take steps to inform all likely objectors. After a time the plans, and the objections to them, will be considered by the borough planning committee. They may decide to grant it outline planning approval. All this takes time and considerable bureaucratic effort. However, in the case of a 'superstore' the plan will also have to go before the GLC planning committee (because of the effect the development might have on neighbouring boroughs) and be subjected to further delay and inquiry.

Under the proposed new arrangements for local government in London this second stage would be eliminated, the boroughs having sole responsibility for approving the plan or rejecting it. So there seems little doubt that many of the thousand or so GLC planners and architects will be facing redundancy if the County Hall layer of government goes.

The government is also looking for real savings in the members of staff who at present form the central administration of the GLC. The thinking here is that most of the GLC staff who actually provide a service to the public, such as the GLC firemen (now labelled in non-sexist terms as 'firefighters'), the GLC building inspectors, the GLC park keepers and so on, will mostly be absorbed into the borough council staff, or into the staff of some of the other 'boards'. This will leave a central core of administrators who will no longer be needed: the secretaries, the finance officers and the personnel managers.

This assumption is also probably true. But allowance has to be made for extra staff to be taken on by the so-called 'successor authorities'. This is where the Department of the Environment estimates and those of the GLC begin to part company. The GLC points to the evidence that reorganization of local government has in the past tended to result in more rather than fewer local government jobs. And in the case of the government's proposals there are provisions for the creation of some five new successor organizations to take over some of the GLC functions. This new, and arguably more complicated, structure could risk replacing one kind of duplication for another. At the moment any doubling up of functions could be described as 'horizontal', with the upper and lower tiers of local government covering the same ground. In the proposed new structure this could become 'vertical' duplication, because each successor body will require its own management hierarchy and its own bureaucracy. In addition to this the GLC has argued that the 'fragmentation' of services and responsibilities will create a need for increased consultation and create the opportunity for more disagreement. This process could both require extra staff and create costly delays.

While the government's financial predictions rest very heavily on the staffing implications of the reform, the GLC has concentrated more on the extra costs that could come from a loss in the 'economy of scale'. In an era in which 'small is beautiful' has become an increasingly popular concept, these claims may well be treated with some scepticism. There is, however, no questioning of the fact that the £2 billion GLC debt has been financed on very favourable terms because of County Hall's apparent financial strength. Borough councils in future will be required to pay more for any further borrowings. It may seem a mundane point, but the GLC finance officers estimate that this could amount in itself to an extra £15 million a year should County Hall go. Another £5 million of extra costs could arise, they argue, from the need to reorganize and re-equip should the central GLC computer network be broken up.

In the last analysis it is impossible to decide, on the basis of the government and GLC calculations, which is more likely to be correct. They simply do not look at the same things. But it is fair to say that the only independent studies made of the government plan have not found the 'rationalization savings' that Kenneth Baker so confidently predicts.

One of these was carried out by a highly respected City firm of consultants, Coopers and Lybrand. They looked not at the GLC plan but at the similar proposals for the abolition of the metropolitan county councils; but their conclusions could almost certainly apply to London too.

Coopers and Lybrand did find evidence that savings could be made in the areas of planning and central administration, just as the government is predicting. But they concluded that these savings would be more than offset by the extra costs incurred in running the services that would have to be re-allocated to the lower-tier borough or district councils. This would be especially true where a great deal of cooperation between councils, probably with sharply opposed political policies, would be required. Two illustrations should be enough to highlight the danger that, in those areas, less efficient practices would creep in.

The first of these concerns the question of major road im-provement and the planning of traffic, a problem common to all the English conurbations. Under the government's plan councils should join together to coordinate work on major roads that cross council boundaries; this would be done using a 'voluntary joint committee' approach. But Coopers and Lybrand found that this idea had been tried in the past and found wanting. A 'West Midlands Traffic Management Committee', represent-ing the six borough councils in the area, had been set up in 1968. It had soon become a parade ground for conflicting interests. When it was wound up in 1974 it had very little to show for its years of effort. This contrasted very sharply with the record of the West Midlands Metropolitan County Council that had stepped into the committee's shoes and actually got things done. A reversion to the old system, Coopers and Lybrand reckoned, was almost certainly going to slow up decision-making and add further to costs through the loss of the economies of scale.

The study also looked at the likely effect of handing over the organization of waste disposal to the lower-tier councils, again on the understanding that some joint cooperation would be worked out. Disposing of the household refuse generated by a conurbation of millions of people is a major undertaking costing, in London, some £66 million a year. This is one reason why most observers assumed that the government would choose to put it on a 'joint-board' footing, maintaining it as one single big operation similar to the Fire Brigade. Instead the Depart-ment of Environment has plumped for the risky option of leaving the whole matter to be sorted out by the borough (or district) councils themselves. Just how much of a gamble this is can be

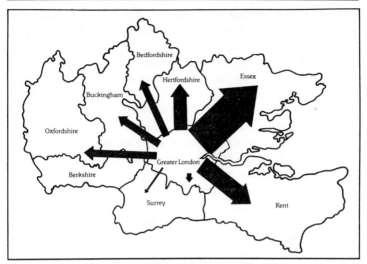

WASTE DISPOSAL BY THE GLC

appreciated by taking only a cursory look at the present scale of the London waste disposal arrangements (see figure). Rubbish from the capital is at present dumped into 'land-fill' sites spread over seven counties and demands the coordination of a huge road, rail and river barge operation. Disputes between individual borough councils on planning and paying for the service seem likely to be all too common. Coopers and Lybrand, looking at the less complex problems found in the 'mets', were forced to conclude that the waste disposal arrangements were likely to be less efficient and more costly, especially if councils could not agree a common policy and decided to go their own way. (The government obviously shared some of these anxieties by providing for the minister to step in, if need be, to establish an alternative arrangement of his own.)

Looking across the whole range of metropolitan county services, Coopers and Lybrand summed up the likely effects of abolition on the efficiency of local government in terms that did not flatter the government's plans: 'there are unlikely to be any net savings as a result of the structural changes proposed by the government ... There could be significant extra costs.' Neither Patrick Jenkin nor Kenneth Baker has ever replied directly to the findings of Coopers and Lybrand, and this has been seen by opponents of abolition as an admission on the government's part that it has lost the argument about how efficient the new post-GLC local council set-up is likely to be. The charge that costs, far from falling, will actually go up as a result of the changes is certainly one to which a Thatcher administration is peculiarly sensitive. Memories of the increased rate bills that followed the last big-shake-up of local government in 1974 (also a Conservative measure) continue to haunt the corridors of Whitehall and account for the controversial decision to give the Secretary of State for the Environment draconian powers to control both the manpower and the spending of the new joint boards and the new ILEA for the first three years of their existence. But if Coopers and Lybrand are correct in their analysis the real cost increases are likely to come in precisely those areas that are not covered by the government controls.

'Policy savings'

If the government's 'rationalization savings' seem unlikely to materialize, there remains a second area of potential economy that cannot be so easily discounted, that described by Kenneth Baker as 'policy savings'. The Tory critique of the present GLC is based as much on the waste that is perceived to arise from 'unnecessary' GLC spending as a result of misguided policies, as it is on the alleged inefficiency of the County Hall bureaucratic and administrative machine. In the Thatcher book the GLC is classed as a massive 'overspender'. Its presumed profligacy derives equally from the ease with which it can raise money and from its present political orientation. A penny rate, raised across the GLC area, produces nearly £20 million. In the view of many Tories that sort of power poses too much of a temptation simply to spend money like water. (It seems that few things are likely to rile government supporters more than to hear Ken Livingstone describe, as he did in October 1984, the £7 million then spent on GLC publicity and propaganda as 'peanuts'.)

Included within the government estimates on 'policy savings' were references not only to the huge advertising budget but to the 'needless extravagance' associated with many GLC

Ken Livingstone sorts out petitions calling for the GLC to be saved.
This was only part of a campaign that would cost £11 million.

committees. A special mention was reserved for the 'Women's Committee', whose budget for looking after the interests of London women was over nine million pounds, a sum – as the statement drily put it – 'three times the budget of the Equal Opportunities Commission', the national body with a similar remit.

But other GLC spending could have been singled out. In the financial year 1983–4 the council devoted some £180 million to subsidizing London Transport, roughly double what the government thought was necessary. In the same year it spent £31 million on job-creation exercises masterminded by the Greater London Enterprise Board (or GLEB), expenditure thought by the Treasury to be positively harmful. Increasing the GLC rates to subsidize 'uneconomic' jobs offended every tenet of Thatcherite free-market economics: it put 'good' jobs at risk, so it was argued, all to try to prop up jobs in declining industries or to provide unwise investment for new projects that could not convince bankers that they had viable prospects.

The list of GLC spending projects that would be classed by the government as reckless is very long indeed. It includes not only the Women's Committee, transport subsidies and GLEB investments but spending on such things as anti-nuclear weapons propaganda, gay and lesbian causes, and the GLC Police Committee, which devoted its considerable energies and cash to monitoring the Metropolitan Police Force.

Viewed like this, the abolition of the GLC would be bound to lead to substantial savings by eliminating such 'extravagance'. With County Hall gone the power to raise the cash would go too, leaving behind a lower-spending and more 'cost-effective' local government in the capital.

But 'policy savings' may not be seen in quite the same light by all the citizens of London. Many of the policies followed by Ken Livingstone's GLC, such as the attempt to keep fares down to encourage greater use of public transport, are by no means the exclusive reserve of left-wing politicians. The work of GLEB has many antecedents: the decline of the London economy has been a major policy concern of both Labour and Conservative GLCs since the mid-seventies. GLEB may be more dogmatic in its approach than previous job initiatives but its work lies in what has become a mainstream of local government policy in this country. Such 'policy savings' could therefore be considered as acting against the efficiency of London as a whole if they should lead to larger traffic jams and longer dole queues.

There is a further area of concern about the abolition proposals that has touched even the government. This is the problem that some highly non-controversial GLC spending could, inadvertently, be brought to a highly unpopular halt. Since 1981 the GLC has hugely expanded its spending on grants to voluntary organizations. Occasionally the popular press has seized on this to ridicule County Hall's Labour leadership. One grant, to an organization called 'Babies against the Bomb', was seized upon as typical of the extravagance of the Ken Livingstone team. Others, to gay and lesbian groups, also merited a special mention. Publicity of this sort convinced many Tory critics that the GLC had become a hopelessly out-of-control grant-donating machine, the sooner got rid of the better. Much to the surprise of the civil servants who put together the original White Paper, the DoE found itself bombarded by hundreds of anxious submissions from such worthwhile bodies as Mencap and Age Concern, who saw the loss of GLC support as a disaster. It then emerged that over 95 per cent of GLC grants were going to such utterly respectable and cost-effective organizations (so cost-effective that the government has been anxious to encourage their development).

Since then the government has been trying to find some mechanism that would ensure the continuation of grants to the voluntary sector after the GLC has gone. Many of these organizations do not operate on the basis of the borough boundaries and are heavily concentrated in Central London. So the Local Government Bill proposes a somewhat primitive all-London arrangement. A borough council which wants to make a grant to an organization that has a cross-borough field of operations can approach the other 31 boroughs (plus the City Corporation) to ask them to share the cost. If two-thirds or more agree it can then 'recover an appropriate portion of the grants, and other expenditure incurred' from each of the other councils.

How this would work out in practice nobody can say, but the experts in the field are far from confident that major damage to some promising projects could be avoided. Most at risk would be organizations like 'Dial-a-Ride', which has built up a much-praised network of minibus services for disabled people across London. At the moment it is entirely funded by the GLC to the tune of $£3\frac{1}{2}$ million pounds per annum. Nicholas Hinton, Director of the National Council for Voluntary Organizations, commented on the LWT 'London Programme Special' last October that

Unless Dial-a-Ride could get the vast majority of London boroughs to contribute towards its services, and go on having to do that year after year after year ... their chances of being able to continue the excellent services they are now providing are slim.

So the 'efficiency' debate is a very complex one. It involves a consideration not just of 'rationalization' and 'policy' savings but of the unforeseen consequences of breaking up the GLC.

It could be further widened to take in consideration of the effect produced by the present GLC function of raising most of its revenue from the City of London and the City of Westminster (because of the very high rateable value of the central business areas) and spending it across the whole of London. To a large extent the government has preserved this by deciding to keep the ILEA, but some of the poorer boroughs still look likely to suffer some financial loss.

In the end we must conclude that the arguments over efficiency cannot be objectively resolved. They depend on political judgement of what is and is not necessary as well as detailed cost-benefit analysis of the proposals. On the whole, however, the government has not yet succeeded in making its case.

More or less democratic?

In the battle for the hearts and minds of Londoners it is not, however, the question of efficiency but that of democracy that has really held the centre of the stage. The GLC publicity machine has cleverly concentrated on the theme that Londoners, no less than citizens of any other town, should have their own council to speak for them, to defend their interests and, ultimately, to submit itself for their endorsement or rejection. 'Say No to No Say' represents a brilliant PR encapsulation of the most powerful argument for something like the GLC. But it inevitably glosses over some of the more complicated problems that face anyone trying to reach a considered judgement on the merits and demerits of the government plan in terms of improving local democracy in London.

There have always been disagreements about what terms like 'London' or 'Greater London' really mean. Everybody agrees that Westminster and Chelsea form part of London. So equally do Limehouse and Battersea. But when it comes to places like Bromley (Kent) and Twickenham (Middlesex), opinions are very much more divided (perhaps if the Post Office had ever got round to changing postal addresses a real London identity in such places might have grown more quickly). If we cannot define who is a Londoner then precisely what does the term 'a voice for London' really mean?

Just as fundamental as what definition of London we decide to adopt is the whole question of whether any real community of interest can stretch across an area as wide as that of the present GLC. The 'localist' view of London still has its champions. They may no longer see the capital as 'a collection of villages' but they would maintain that London is better understood and better administered as a 'confederation of communities' rather than as a single unit. This is a view quite anathema to 'centralists', who argue that the whole conurbation has to be seen as a single unit if certain common 'metropolitan' problems are ever to be given the priority they deserve. Attempts to reconcile such diametrically opposed conceptions of the capital have, up to now, never really succeeded in producing a satisfactory democratic framework for local government in London.

The proposals now before parliament, if passed, would represent a decided lurch in the direction of localism. Its supporters also argue that it would improve the workings of local democracy by making it more easily understood and more accountable. The present division of local government services in London between the borough councils and the GLC is certainly the source of great confusion and is difficult for the citizen to understand. One London Tory MP tells the story of a loyal party supporter who approached him at a Conservative social gathering to say how enthusiastic he was about knocking Ken Livingstone from his throne and stemming the flood of County Hall propaganda. He was, however, worried about one important little detail. 'When the GLC goes,' he enquired with just a hint of anxiety, 'who will empty my dustbins?' (He had apparently never realized that refuse collection in London is the responsibility of the London boroughs.)

If electors cannot grasp which council is responsible for which service in the present two-tier system it is hard to argue that it is really democratically accountable. And study after study has shown that the man in the street, not on the whole fascinated by the political processes of British democracy, has the greatest difficulty in distinguishing one tier from another. As a result all parties have to a greater or lesser degree espoused the cause of one-tier local government. (Both Labour and the Alliance parties are in favour of the idea in principle.) If each citizen has only one local council, responsible for all the local government services, then he or she knows where to turn to when those services are needed and whom to blame when things are not as they should be. Under the Thatcher/Jenkin plan there would be in fact only one elected local council in each part of London. Because of this new simplicity, it is argued, local democracy will function more effectively. Patrick Jenkin put the point as forcibly as he could in his foreword to the 'Yellow Paper' published in July 1984 to put the finishing touches to the government's plan. Taking a swipe at the highly successful GLC advertising campaign, he wrote:

contrary to the impression given by recent misleading advertising, almost all the functions [of the GLC] will devolve, either individually or jointly, on to the local, democratically elected, councils – in London the London borough councils.

This meant, he said, that local government would be closer to the people:

Abolition will therefore mean the decentralization of powers to the local level ... It will bring benefits also to the users of local services because the councils responsible for these services will be more accessible and more responsive to their needs.

This was, in short, the chief government argument that the abolition of the GLC, far from being an attack on local democracy, actually improved on what had gone before. It ran, as we will see, into a storm of criticism. But by August the government had acquired a second string to its 'better democracy' bow, and an extremely powerful one. This was due to its change of mind about the Inner London Education Authority. *Streamlining the Cities*, the White Paper that first put flesh on the government's scheme for London, had proposed a new 'joint board' to run the ILEA. Under pressure from Sir Keith Joseph this huge organization, which had a budget larger than that of all the rest of the GLC departments put together, was now to become a directly elected education authority in its own right, with its elections to be held every four years concurrently with the borough council elections. Under the present arrangements, the ILEA has had a unique constitution that has tended to blur its lines of democratic accountability. It is officially a subcommittee of the GLC, but its governing body consists of the inner London GLC members and a borough council appointee from each of the inner London boroughs. To make matters more confusing it prepares its budget separately from the GLC itself and issues its own rate demands (or precept) on the boroughs. The existing ILEA structure has been heavily criticized in the past, particularly by Conservative borough councils in inner London. Sir Frank Marshall, who prepared a report on the GLC for the Cutler adminstration, commented:

The chief cause of concern is that because of the ILEA's constitutional status it has an entrenched financial position which, with no provision for democratic challenge either by the GLC or the Boroughs, provides it, at least in theory, with an open cheque-book ... it would clearly be more healthy both for the education service itself and for local government generally if there could be found a more direct means by which the Authority justified its budget to those who had to pay for it.

Sir Frank was not considering the future of the ILEA in the context of an abolition of the GLC, and his preferred solution was not direct election to the ILEA but passing it over to be run by the inner London boroughs. Nevertheless, his report highlighted the weaknesses in the existing ILEA structure. The government can claim, with some justification, that the new ILEA will be more democratic and more easily understood than the present almost Byzantine arrangements. But it rather spoils its image as a champion of local democracy by its decision to subject the new education authority to direct central government control of both manpower levels and budget for its first three years of existence.

Many opponents of the government consider that its stance on local democracy is essentially a bogus one, lacking in all credibility. After all, the same government is responsible for the introduction of ratecapping, a measure its opponents see as introducing an unprecedented degree of central government interference in the day-to-day operation of local government. In the eyes of the opposition parties the proposed abolition of the GLC is consistent with the government's strategy elsewhere.

ABOLITION OF THE GLC – Government Proposals for Reallocating Functions

JOINT BOARDS	FIRE AND CIVIL DEFENCE		
ELECTED BODY	INNER LONDON EDUCATION AUTHORITY		
NON-ELECTED BODIES or 'QUANGOS'	ARTS COUNCIL (PART)	LONDON PLANNING COMMISSION	LONDON RESIDUARY BODY DEBT/PENSIONS
SPECIAL JOINT ARRANGEMENTS	TRAFFIC MANAGEMENT *	CROSS-BOROUGH PLANNING	WASTE DISPOSAL *
BOROUGHS	PLANNING **	ASSISTANCE TO INDUSTRY	BUILDING CONTROL
DIRECT GOVERNMENT CONTROL	MAJOR ROADS		

* *Ministerial 'Reserve' Powers*　　　** *Subject to Ministerial 'guidance'*

Some GLC responsibilities may in fact pass from County Hall directly to the borough councils, but they amount to very little. The important remaining GLC 'metropolitan' functions, on the other hand, are to pass into the hands of non-elected bodies or to central government itself. The outcome, so the critics say, will be to leave Londoners in the unenviable position of having very little say in the running of their own city.

London, even at the moment, is very badly off compared with other urban areas in Britain. It has no semblance of local democratic control over its own police force. It has never controlled its own water supplies. Since the early seventies it has lost control over its own sewers to the Thames Water

STORIC UILDINGS AND USEUM COMMISSION	SPORTS COUNCIL (PART)	THAMES WATER AUTHORITY	LONDON REGIONAL TRANSPORT

RANTS TO OLUNTARY ODIES	PARKS (PART)

RADING ANDARDS	OTHER SERVICES ***	SPORT (PART)	ARTS (PART)	HIGHWAYS **	PARKS (PART)

***   *Includes Archaeology, Archives, Coroners, Probation Officers, some Grants, Public Safety, Tourism.*

Authority and of its own buses and tubes to the new London Regional Transport. If the Thatcher/Jenkin proposals were ever to pass on to the Statute Book, the opposition parties now maintain, the last remnants of democratic control over the 'metropolitan' London-wide issues would be stripped away.

The government has forcefully contested these claims. Kenneth Baker, speaking on an LWT 'London Programme Special' in October 1984, stated unequivocally that on abolition of the GLC 'Some 75 per cent of the GLC's expenditure is going straight to the London boroughs and the balance, which is the Fire Board, will actually be controlled by the borough councillors.' This is very hard to reconcile with the claim, made by Ken Livingstone on the same programme, that '70 or 80 per cent of what the GLC currently does is not going to the boroughs.'

So where precisely does the truth lie? Both sides agree that the London Fire Brigade is not to become a directly run borough service, but they differ radically on who is going to control it. It will be run by the one true 'joint board' to be set up in London under the plan. Just how democratic it will be is subject to the fiercest disagreement. The 'Save the GLC' campaigners have tended to lump it along with 'quangos' as an unaccountable body. They also stress that there will be strict government control over its budget for three years (just like the ILEA). In addition they can cite academic research that has looked at the workings of joint boards in the past. Although joint boards consist of nominated councillors coming from each local council within their areas of responsibility, a study by Norman Flynn and Steve Leach prepared for the Institute of Local Government Studies in Birmingham found that members of past joint boards 'maintained only the loosest of links with parent authorities' and 'were dominated by the professional officers who administer the service controlled by the board'. More controversially, Flynn and Leach went on to predict that any new joint board as proposed in the government scheme could easily become a vehicle for central government control through a combination of apathy and internal division:

Agendas would be thin, except at crucial moments, and attendances low. Where crucial decisions were required and could not be reached amongst the districts (boroughs), influence over these decisions would tend to flow upwards to ... central government.

So while Kenneth Baker might choose to consider the proposed 'Joint Fire Board' as an example of borough control, Ken Livingstone could equally argue that it was nothing of the sort. Nevertheless, it would perhaps be going too far to see the Fire Board as the touchstone of any debate on democratic accountability. The Fire Service is already subject to Home Office supervision and is, in any case, unlikely to throw up major controversies. The critics are on far stronger ground when they point to the number of County Hall services that will pass (or have already passed) not to joint boards but to government-appointed bodies. The loss of London Transport services to the new London Regional Transport has already taken place. By means of a piece of mental fast footwork the government has left LRT out of any calculation about which GLC service goes where. It holds to the view that the decision to remove the running of London's tubes and buses from County Hall control has nothing whatever to do with the present abolition plans – except in so far as it underlines the growing redundancy of the GLC. Since Londoners are still obliged to provide a subsidy to LRT through their rates bill, most people will continue to assume that transport is a local government service that has been removed to non-elected control. (The dispute over the classification of transport partly accounts for the huge discrepancy between Department of the Environment and County Hall figures on the borough council share of ex-GLC services.)

There certainly can be no argument over the GLC services still to be transferred to the so-called quangos. (LRT might, loosely speaking, also be considered as a quango rather than a nationalized industry.) Quangos are fundamentally undemocratic in operation, and the loss of services to them cannot be defended as an improvement in local democracy. But the government can fairly point out that, together, they represent only 7 per cent of the present GLC budget. They might have argued that such duties as running the Thames Flood Barrier or the South Bank arts complex are not political issues as such, but that has to be questioned in the light of the distinctive left-wing GLC policy of 'bringing art to the people' which has not only questioned artistic values but also raised the issue of the balance to be struck between subsidizing prestigious South Bank productions and the promotion of 'popular theatre' out in the community.

On issues like these the government seems prepared to put up with any flak that comes its way. As an issue the increased role of quangos such as the Arts Council or the Historic Buildings and Monuments Commission in post-GLC London is not likely to prove a stumbling block to the passing of the Local Government Bill now before parliament. What would be far more of a problem as far as the 'democracy' debate is concerned are certain provisions within the Bill that claim to be doing one thing but, on closer examination, seem likely to achieve something quite radically different. For critics maintain that the threat to local democracy runs far deeper than any casual reading of the Bill would suggest.

Hidden centralization?

One such 'grey area' concerns the future of traffic control across the capital. It is one area in which the GLC, with its computer-controlled traffic light system and some neatly contrived traffic management schemes, has a fairly good record. On reading the Local Government Bill it seems that these powers will pass directly to the boroughs. This will be done by amending the Traffic Acts of 1972 and 1984. As the Bill puts it: '... the principal purpose of the amendments being to transfer functions ... from the Greater London Council to London borough councils ...'

It seems simple enough until it is actually related to the London scene. It is fairly obvious that the flow of traffic through one borough is critically affected by the policies towards traffic pursued by its neighbouring borough councils. When the White Paper came out in October 1983 it stressed that 'traffic matters will require close co-operation between borough councils ...' generally to be done through 'voluntary joint committees'. It was assumed that traffic management would be largely non-controversial and that even councils of different political complexions could work together. But within a few weeks this assumption was shown up to be hopelessly naive. A simple matter of a 'contraflow' bus lane in central London brought out into the open the underlying tensions between neighbouring boroughs. Camden, under solid Labour control and favouring public transport, had submitted a proposal to the GLC designed to improve access for shoppers to the busy Oxford Street shopping area. Buses coming into central London from Camden at present are diverted down a one-way system that runs the length of Gower Street, leaving shoppers with some way to walk. The council's proposal was for a 'contraflow' bus lane to run southwards down Tottenham Court Road to Centrepoint, allow-

IF YOU HAVE ANY COMPLAINTS WHEN THE GLC GOES, YOU'LL BE TALKING TO WHITEHALL.

SAY NO TO NO SAY.

This product of the 'Save the GLC' campaign cleverly avoided defining what the GLC actually did, in favour of portraying the civil service as unsympathetic to problems in general.

ing passenger set-down at the end of Oxford Street itself. As chance would have it the boundary between Camden and the Conservative-controlled Westminster met at Centrepoint. Westminster was, as a council, more on the side of the private motorist and the business traveller. It viewed the Camden proposal as totally wrong-headed: it was bound to restrict the heavy flow of traffic that went northwards up Tottenham Court Road, causing it to tail back into Westminster itself. At the moment the final decision is left to the GLC but, people asked, what would happen after the GLC had gone? The Tottenham Court Road controversy may be an extreme example, but it is only one of many disputes that are likely to arise if the boroughs are left to their own devices.

Clearly the government could not be saddled with an unworkable scheme when it came to be debated in parliament. It had already acknowledged that the Department of Transport might have to get involved to some degree. But during the consultation period it was decided to define the powers of the Secretary of State for Transport (the government minister concerned) much more clearly in order to resolve any disputes of the Tottenham Court Road variety. The 'Yellow Paper', when it appeared in July, categorically stated that 'Where disputes cannot be settled by the parties themselves, the Secretary of

IF THE GLC GOES, WHITEHALL MOVES IN.

London is better off run by Londoners, not Whitehall. **SAY NO TO NO SAY.**

The suggestion that Whitehall was snail-like in its decision-making annoyed civil servants at the DoE. But this poster sought to capitalize on the poor public image of the Whitehall bureaucracy.

State's consent will be needed before the proposal can go ahead.'

But the 'Yellow Paper' went much further than this. Perhaps it had occurred to someone in the Transport Ministry that the GLC might rush through a number of controversial bus-lane schemes. The Secretary of State was now to be given the power to issue 'guidelines' to borough councils to provide what was called 'an overall context'. These 'guidelines', however, had all the makings of an order. Should any council use its option not to follow them, the Secretary of State was to have 'reserve powers' to act. Admittedly the minister could do so only if there were likely to be *'adverse consequences'* for traffic (our emphasis). But these 'adverse consequences' were defined in the Bill as 'an adverse effect on the regulation of traffic', so hopelessly vague and subjective a definition as to give the minister virtual *carte blanche*.

In the field of traffic management it seems that the passing of control 'down to the boroughs' would be largely an illusion. The Bill even provided for the minister to run the traffic lights system where he considered arrangements between boroughs to be 'inadequate'. If necessary the Secretary of State could 'install, maintain, alter or remove, or otherwise manage traffic signs'. If these 'reserve powers' were ever to be used – and that seemed very likely in the context of squabbling London

Ken Livingstone with Labour Leader Neil Kinnock and pensioners' leader Jack Jones at County Hall Christmas Party for pensioners, 1984.

boroughs – civil servants in Whitehall would find themselves involved in the day-to-day running of the capital in a totally unprecedented way.

It is possible to detect a certain tension between the Department of the Environment, which carries overall responsibility for the Bill, and the Department of Transport. The Department of the Environment people view the 'interventionist' flavour of the Department of Transport road engineers with a certain disdain. So it is worth pointing out that some other sections of the Bill, not prepared by the Department of Transport, imply an almost equally strong ministerial role in a post-GLC London. Clause 3(1) deals with town planning and states clearly that 'the Council of a London borough is the local planning authority for the borough'. But the bald statement will again be no guarantee of borough independence to act on its own. For tucked away in Schedule 1 it is specified that the borough council 'shall have regard . . . to any strategic advice by the Secretary of State'.

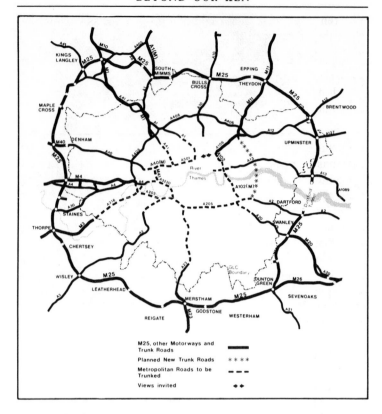

PROPOSED TRUNK ROAD NETWORK IN LONDON
The broken lines indicate GLC roads that will pass to the Department
of Transport under Government plans.

The Secretary of State (to be advised in turn by a new quango,
'the London Planning Commission') is, however, in a much
stronger position than the word 'advice' would suggest. Under
planning law he has the right to accept or reject any plan drawn
up by the borough. This is a power he may wish to use sparingly
but, in a London no longer with any overall planning authority,
he could find himself sucked into the detailed planning process.
This is certainly the view of a study made by planning profes-
sionals and academics for an LSE/University College London

Conference in April 1984. Examining the government plan in detail, they concluded that

the proposals appear to carry advantages over the present system *but only if the Secretary of State is not drawn in, politically*, to detailed borough development issues. *Such intervention is, also, highly likely.* (Our emphasis)

As far as local democracy is concerned, then it could be fair to conclude that there is a considerable gulf between the stated intentions of the government's Local Government Bill and its likely outcome in practice. Patrick Jenkin's claim in the 'Yellow Paper' that 'Abolition will mean the decentralization of powers to local level' would seem to have a certain hollow ring. Perhaps he would have been better advised to acknowledge from the outset that many of the 'strategic' powers of the GLC (powers which in many cases the GLC had not wielded very effectively) could not be passed to the individual boroughs. It could have been argued that, in a capital city, it was perfectly proper for central government to assume a direct interest. This position was, after all, adopted from the start in relation to the 70 miles of GLC main roads (including the South Circular Road) that, under the plan, will pass directly into the hands of the Secretary of State for Transport. Central government is, of course, directly accountable to parliament. In the House of Commons the London MPs would then have the role of defending the democratic rights of Londoners.

As it is, 'creeping centralization' will continue to be highlighted in parliament and, try as it might, the government will inevitably be depicted as attempting to deprive Londoners of their democratic rights by a sinister and underhand device. While the debate could have centred on the role of parliament as a democratic watchdog, it is instead the brick-wall image of the Whitehall civil servant, so cleverly exploited by the GLC in its publicity campaign, that will remain uppermost in the public mind.

'When the GLC goes, Whitehall moves in' is not, of course, the only slogan that has had a bearing on the 'democracy' debate. Even more potent is the idea that, should the GLC be abolished, there will no longer be 'a voice for London'. This notion is most strongly articulated in the claim that London will be the only capital city in the Western world without its own elected council. It is in dealing with charges of this nature that the government has been at its most uncomfortable. Attempts to ward off the criticism by pointing out that the Paris City Council has its responsibilities confined to only a small fraction of the Paris conurbation – the historic central core – has been of no use when it is pointed out that the City of London (which might be seen as an equivalent) has virtually no population and a totally archaic system of elections: the Lord Mayor of London cannot rank with the Mayor of Paris as a spokesman for the popular interest. Nor have arguments that the GLC speaks only for those Londoners who voted for the majority party at County Hall been any more effective; by the same token Mrs Thatcher can never claim to 'speak for Britain'.

Just how weak a position the government was in on this issue was demonstrated by a large-scale rebellion among its own backbenchers last December. When the Local Government Bill entered its short committee stage on the floor of the House an opposition amendment to preserve some kind of assembly for Greater London was only narrowly defeated. The government majority, nominally 142, fell to only 23.

Is there another way?

Had the amendment been carried it would have also committed the government to the setting up of a new inquiry into the future of London government. By the spring of 1984, it seemed that the government might have been better advised to have done this in the first place. In 1983 there was a widespread acceptance that the GLC/borough arrangement was not working properly and that some changes were necessary. But the government failed to appreciate that the abolition of the Greater London Council was a much more complex undertaking than might be imagined. The government scheme, on balance, seems unlikely to improve the efficiency of local government in the capital. As far as democratic accountability is concerned, while there are some improvements (especially as concerned the ILEA), the new structure looks unworkable without a significant increase in central government involvement in London affairs. Traditionally Tories have been suspicious of any accretion of power to the centre. Now they are being asked to swallow a new system of ministerial control that could, in the hands of a left-wing government, threaten the very interests they have sought to protect.

In the light of the shortcomings of the present Local Government Bill the urge to set up some form of independent inquiry could prove too strong for the House of Lords to resist. In the next few months the growing pressure for such a move must represent the greatest threat to the Thatcher-inspired policy pursued up to now. In the next chapter we will consider what alternative schemes for London government any independent inquiry would be bound to consider.

8. THE BATTLE FOR THE METROPOLITAN COUNTIES

In the government's view there will always be conflicts between those who argue for large-scale organizations on grounds of efficiency and those, on the other hand, who argue for control by a body close to the people for whom the service is designed. (Peter Shore, Environment Secretary, Torquay, 9 June 1978)

Inevitably, much of the debate about abolition centres on London. This is partly because it is one of the world's great capital cities, with a population of just under 7 million. But it is partly also because so many of the people involved in the debate live and work in London – civil servants, national media journalists, parliament are all concentrated there. As the capital, London also has an aspect which is of national interest in a way which does not apply to other major cities in the country.

In addition, the legislative proposals imply the most profound changes in London. Even after abolition major cities like Manchester, Liverpool, Birmingham, Leeds, Newcastle and Sheffield will all have a directly elected city-wide council. London will not. Apart from a directly elected education authority for the inner London area it will have nothing that is both London-wide and directly elected.

But it would be a mistake to assume, therefore, that the abolition of England's six metropolitan county councils, scheduled for the same date as the death of the GLC, is neither important nor controversial.

The way in which the metropolitan counties were set up in 1974 caused deep annoyance among the populations involved; the way in which they are being dismantled is equally contentious. Indeed, although the changes affect, in total, only seven councils (including the GLC), these authorities cover a quarter of the entire population of Britain. And what was wrongly interpreted by the Conservatives as legislation likely to meet with popular approbation could turn into an electoral disadvantage across a great swathe of England.

The 1974 reforms

Local government changes have a habit of irritating people. In 1974 people who had always lived in Somerset suddenly found themselves in a new county: Avon. Bournemouth 'appeared' in Dorset although everybody then knew, as they know now, that it is really part of Hampshire. Rutland disappeared, although its alarmed and protesting inhabitants (and its dukedom, created in 1703) survived.

Part of this unpopular movement of people and places which

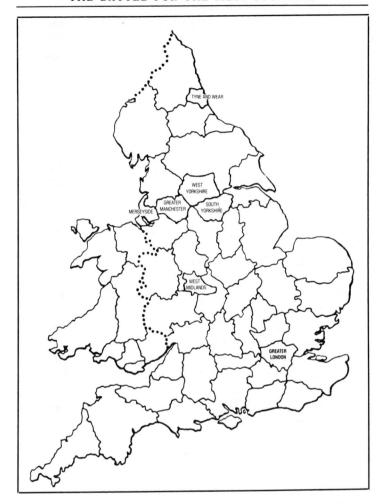

METROPOLITAN COUNTIES IN ENGLAND AND WALES

were not keen to be displaced involved the creation of the six metropolitan county councils: Greater Manchester, Merseyside, South Yorkshire, Tyne and Wear, West Midlands and West Yorkshire. It is worth looking briefly at how this came about.

As we have seen, commissions and committees have sat on and off throughout this century trying to decide how best to organize devolved government in Britain. Yet there has always been a feeling that the status quo, whatever it happens to be, is not quite right.

This was thought to be especially so in England and Wales, where the pattern had been established at the end of the nineteenth century and many county boundaries had been drawn in the Middle Ages. Although some 20 new county boroughs were created between 1888 and 1929 and some changes were made to urban boundaries before the 1939–45 war, the structure of local government was largely hopelessly out of date by the 1960s, having been overtaken by population growth and movement and industrial changes, notably in transportation. So the largest county – Lancashire – had a population 80 times larger than the smallest – Rutland. The county borough of Birmingham was 30 times bigger than that of Canterbury, and so on. Absurdities were the rule rather than the exception.

To deal with all this in provincial England a new Royal Commission was established in 1966 under the chairmanship of Lord Redcliffe-Maud (chairman of the earlier Maud Commitee on local authorities' internal management). It was required.

to consider the structure of local government in England, outside Greater London, in relation to its existing functions; and to make recommendations for authorities and boundaries, and for functions and their division, having regard to the size and the character of areas in which these can be most effectively exercised and the need to sustain a viable system of democracy.

It sat for three years, reporting in July 1969 after taking a mass of evidence, largely from vested interests. It found six fundamental problems:

● the division between town and country

● the division between county boroughs and counties

● the division of responsibility within counties

● the small size of many authorities

● the relationship between local authorities and the public

● the relationship between local authorities and central government.

The commission (with an important dissenting report by Derek Senior) proposed that most of provincial England should be divided into 58 unitary multiservice authorities, covering town and rural areas with the major towns as focal points. Populations of more than 1 million were undesirable, so for the three largest conurbations a London-type solution was proposed, with two tiers of local government: the districts and three metropolitan top-tier authorities – West Midlands, Merseyside and SelNec (South East Lancashire and North East Cheshire). The top tier would have dealt with transport, planning, water, sewerage, refuse disposal, police, fire and ambulance. Housing and recreation would have been shared services with 20 metropolitan districts which would have sole responsibility for all other services, including the crucial education service. The commission also proposed eight indirectly elected provincial councils as major strategic authorities.

The Labour government's response in a White Paper in February 1970 was partially faithful to Redcliffe-Maud but added two more top-tier metropolitan counties – South Hampshire, covering Southampton and Portsmouth, and West Yorkshire. Most significantly, it also proposed to take education in these areas up to metropolitan county level.

Harold Wilson then lost the 1970 election and the concept of unitary authorities went down with him, having attracted a very hostile reaction from Tories. Mr Heath's incoming team, still largely 'big is beautiful' corporatists – especially Peter Walker, the new Environment Secretary – discarded Labour's plans and produced its own bigger and more 'beautiful' proposals, which discarded South Hampshire but invented new metropolitan counties for South Yorkshire and Tyne and Wear. So there would now be six large conurbation authorities rather than Redcliffe-Maud's three and Labour's five, and 36 rather than 20 metropolitan districts. (This was all embodied in the 1972 Local Government Act, which took effect on 1 April 1974, when the new shire districts and counties also came into being.)

By the time the Tories' White Paper was published in February 1971, however, interventions had been made by one of the few doubters about the whole idea: Mrs Margaret Thatcher.

Stimulated by her newly acquired knowledge of the Inner London Education Authority, whose expenditure and education policies had appalled her, she intervened (as we have seen) to prevent Mr Walker from including education as a metropolitan county function, returning it to the district level recommended by Redcliffe-Maud in the first place. The seeds against the large-scale, corporatist approach were already being sown into the fertile soil of Mrs Thatcher's philosophical development and, in this respect at least, she can be regarded as an early radical.

Labour wins the metropolitan counties

Still, the metropolitan county councils stayed fairly well out of Mrs Thatcher's immediate glare during the early part of her first term of office. Rates were still the key problem and annual party conference embarrassment. After all, until 1981 only two of the six metropolitan counties were controlled by Labour councils. They were South Yorkshire and Tyne and Wear – the two the Tories had deliberately invented back in 1974. And in London the Tories also had control of the Greater London Council.

But the storm clouds were gathering. The rates problem was getting more contentious and no solution was in sight. The government's new grant system was not working properly and so arbitrary and unscientific spending targets had to be introduced against which councils were judged for 'overspending' and penalized. The GLC, the ILEA and the metropolitan counties all showed up as high overspenders.

Then, in May 1981, came the blow which was psychologically too much for the prime minister. Labour swept into urban power on Thursday 7 May, winning the GLC and sweeping the metropolitan county council board.

This was, of course, a year before the Falklands War factor changed Mrs Thatcher's fortunes. In 1981 she and her Cabinet were deeply unpopular, the recession was biting hard, the country was disappointed and gloomy. Many urban Labour voters who had clearly voted Tory in 1979 reverted in the local polls of 1981. Outside the urban areas the Tories did badly too, with Labour gaining control of the deep-blue county of

Lancashire, gaining Nottinghamshire and Derbyshire and remarkably ousting the Tories from overall control in Leicestershire, Warwickshire, Northamptonshire and, most astonishingly, Cheshire.

Central Office spirits plummeted as the results came in, reaching a low for the year when the moderate Tory administration in the West Midlands County Council, the country's second largest with 3 million voters, fell to Labour on an exceptionally large overall swing of 18 per cent, which soared to 30 per cent in some parts of the county.

It was not evident at the time, but these results and their future impact on both local government expenditure and the growth of left-wing urban municipal power bases were to be the undoing of the metropolitan county councils. If the Tories had retained just two in 1981 it is doubtful whether, even in the desperate panic to throw something into the 1983 manifesto, the metropolitan county councils would have been nominated for execution.

The government immediately started to look hard at the councils' expenditure and, much later, at their functions. Within two weeks of the May 1981 local elections a large *ad hoc* Cabinet committee gathered to approve a total of £900 million in grant penalties for overshooting of 1981–2 targets.

High among the worst overspenders were three metropolitan county councils – South Yorkshire (£22.28 million or 17.8 per cent over target), West Yorkshire (£22.41 million or 13.3 per cent over target) and Merseyside (£19.34 million or 12.5 per cent over). In fact, local authority budgets are set by March each year so, in the case of West Yorkshire and Merseyside, Labour was not in power when the budgets were set. No matter. They were Labour in May. The axe was out and the battle was on.

The six metropolitan counties accounted for £116.78 million of overspending out of a total £900 million overshoot. The following year councils budgeted to overshoot targets by £1.3 billion, of which £185 million was accounted for by the metropolitan county councils. By 1984–5 the overall local authority budgets were only £848 million above targets, with the metropolitan counties accounting for £58 million.

In fact these targets have been largely discredited and are a constant source of embarrassment to many officials at the Environment Department responsible for assessing local authorities' spending needs. But they have served a useful political purpose because they enabled the word 'overspending' to become part of the vocabulary in the local government debate, making it easier for the government to imply that profligacy, particularly on the part of Labour councils, was causing very high rate increases.

CHANGES IN RATE BILLS AND AVERAGE INCOMES 1978–9 TO 1984–5

	Rate Bills %	Average Incomes %
Greater London	+ 183.6	+ 112.6
West Midlands		+ 94.4
South Yorkshire		+ 90.7
West Yorkshire	+ 165.6	+ 102.1
Greater Manchester		+ 99.4
Merseyside		+ 91.3
Tyne and Wear		+ 95.3
England and Wales	+ 146.9	+ 100.7

A redundant tier?

But the government was not only looking increasingly askance at metropolitan county spending. It was also starting to deploy the argument that the counties represented a redundant tier of government structure which did not do anything useful. In this the government was aided by many of the metropolitan districts, Labour and Tory, which did not like the 'Big Brother' super-councils. If the counties were abolished, many council leaders argued, their district councils would become more important and powerful as they took over their functions. In addition much of the strain which had developed between the two tiers would be eliminated, bureaucracy and duplication would be diminished and efficiency and accountability enhanced.

There is no doubt that in one key respect – planning – this is true. There has been nothing but acrimony in the metropolitan areas over this. The amount of time-wasting, paper-shuffling and argument has had a debilitating effect on all the staff concerned and has been largely due to the inability of parliament to take a sensible view about which planning functions properly lie at which tier of government. The result has been some powers remaining at the centre, others with the county and others with the district, all interlocking and interdependent and with no clear and consistent lines of authority. The trouble caused by this state of planning affairs lies, more than any other single issue, behind the antipathy of the metropolitan district towards the county councils.

However, although the districts will have clearer and enhanced planning powers if the abolition legislation reaches the Statute Book, they will be denied many of the other prizes for which they were hoping. They will get none of the major services. In fact, some 80 per cent by expenditure of all metropolitan county services will go to joint boards, joint committees and quangoes. As the table on pp. 160–1 shows, the three most important services which account for this major share of expenditure – fire, police and transport – all have to go to joint boards. Waste disposal may also have to go to a joint board. The government's critics argue that this very inability of the districts to run any of the principal top-tier services is in itself a rational justification for retaining a directly and democratically elected council to run them, even if planning and most of the 'bits and pieces' are passed down to the lower tier.

Transport has generally been a great success story in terms of upper-tier local government. Tyne and Wear has a metro system which is fast, efficient, economic, well patronized and attracts visits from interested governments and local authority deputations from around the world. It would never have been built by a joint board or joint committee.

South Yorkshire is another example of an authority which

ABOLITION OF THE METROPOLITAN COUNTY COUNCILS – Government Proposals for Reallocation of Functions

JOINT BOARDS	FIRE	POLICE	PUBLIC TRANSPORT		
NON-ELECTED BODIES or 'QUANGOS'	ARTS (PART)	DEBT/ PENSIONS	SPORT (PART)		
SPECIAL JOINT ARRANGEMENTS	GRANTS TO VOLUNTARY BODIES		TRAFFIC MANAGEMENT *		MAIN ROADS
DISTRICT COUNCILS	ARTS (PART)	ASSISTANCE TO INDUSTRY		CIVIL DEFENCE	PLANNIN **

*   *Ministerial 'Reserve' Powers*   **   *Ministerial 'guidance'*

instituted a transport policy right across the conurbation under its control immediately after its creation. The hump of the financial burden of implementing and holding a very low fares policy has long since been passed, so that the county has had a very cheap, very efficient public transportation system which has been heavily used, with the result that there has been remarkably little traffic congestion in major cities like Sheffield.

One problem with transferring transport to a joint board or, as in the case of London, a quango, is that fares policy cannot be tested at the ballot box, although the board and quango can still levy a charge on the ratepayer. If free market economics rather than transport economics are also to apply, the net result can be detrimental to the consumer, who has no redress other than to cease using public transport. In London, for example, the London Regional Transport quango decided to raise London Transport fares by an average 9 per cent in January 1985 *and* to levy a precept of 10.8p in the pound on all London boroughs and, therefore, on all London ratepayers.

Neither the fares levels nor the precepts need to be presented to the electorate as policy at any point. All the joint boards and

WASTE DISPOSAL *	AIRPORTS			

HIGHWAYS **	PARKS	SPORT (PART)	TRADING STANDARDS	OTHER SERVICES ***

*** *Includes Archaeology, Archives, Coroners, Probation Officers, Tourism.*

quangos have similar precepting powers, enabling them to collect money from the boroughs or districts which have, in turn, to collect it from the ratepayers.

A more philosophical problem arises over police forces. In the metropolitan county areas the new proposals will bring them compulsorily under the control of joint boards. The tradition of policing in Britain has always been localist, with forces directly accountable through their chief constables to locally elected police authorities and the Home Secretary accountable to parliament for law and order. Most chief constables prefer the present arrangements and there is little support for the move to a non-accountable joint police board (which is not the same as the voluntary combined police forces in some shire areas such as Avon and Somerset or Devon and Cornwall). At least one chief constable – Sir Philip Knight in the West Midlands – favours smaller police forces rather than large metropolitan forces under the control of widely drawn joint boards. Under his plan there could be a separate police force, for example, for Birmingham City, returning to the arrangements which existed in the old county borough days.

This suggestion highlights one of the major deficiencies of the government's plan: not enough time and consideration has been given to alternative proposals to ensure that what follows is better than what goes.

It might be, for example, that in some areas it would be preferable to abolish the metropolitan county; in others it might be suitable to abolish the county and merge some of the districts; a third possibility might be to consider letting all the districts go other than the major city in some areas.

Tyne and Wear, for example, appears to be a cohesive unit of government covering an area with which its residents clearly identify. Merseyside is a more extreme example. Not only is there very strong regional identification with the area but there is also very little affinity for many of its districts, such as Sefton and Knowsley. There was also widespread support for the metropolitan county council among trade and business organizations, which felt it fulfilled a vital regional role in a deeply depressed part of the country. Even the local chamber of commerce urged its retention, although it lost much of its enthusiasm when the Labour leadership of the county made a serious political miscalculation and disrupted traffic through the Mersey tunnels as part of its protest against government policies towards local government. The amount of goodwill lost by this otherwise ineffective demonstration of political cussedness is incalculable.

Although there is a case to be made against the metropolitan counties, it is not clear that the mixture of joint arrangements and quangos with power to extract money from ratepayers' pockets without being in any way accountable to those ratepayers for spending decisions is a suitable way forward. And it is the small things that will matter as much as the great. West Yorkshire County Council, for instance, has staff and a computer housed in Leeds which controls all the traffic lights in Leeds and Wakefield, linked to another in Bradford, controlling Bradford, Huddersfield and, ultimately, Halifax lights. After abolition who owns the computer, who will run the system, who is going to pay what portion of which costs and to whom?

9. A PAUSE FOR THOUGHT?

It is still not too late to halt the process in order to examine the issues in depth before rushing into another ill-considered reorganization ... The future of the London region and the underlying issues of effective democracy and accountability are surely great enough to warrant thorough analysis. (Alan Norton, speaking at 'Governing London' conference, April 1984)

The Local Government Bill's proposals for the abolition of the Greater London Council and the metropolitan county councils had already received a rough reception in parliament by the beginning of 1985. In particular, a strong and influential body of parliamentary opinion believed the London proposals had too many weaknesses; that the government should pause to consider whether there were better alternatives on offer. The establishment of a Select Committee of MPs or an independent commission of inquiry could stop what many saw as a rush into half-baked reform that would neither work very well nor have much chance of standing the test of time.

Any inquiry of this type could consider the experience of other countries where capital cities and other large conurbations presented similar problems to that of London; it could look at the large number of alternative schemes for a new London local council structure that had poured out of a series of academic and local government conferences; and it could commission research of its own. Given adequate time to gather evidence and to consider its conclusions, such an inquiry should be able to come up with a solution to the acknowledged problems of government in the capital that would be both more efficient and democratically more accountable. This certainly was the hope of those who supported the strategy of a pause for further thought.

But could such an inquiry actually agree on its recommendations? There may be many suitable models for a new London council structure, but they are based on radically different concepts of what the proper concerns of local government should be. Function influences design in local government just as surely as it does in engineering. Unfortunately there is now less agreement than anyone can remember on what local councils should do. At the end of the day it is likely that a preference for one scheme or another will depend less on analysis than on political outlook.

The greatest divide is between those who believe that services and issues that are metropolitan or regional in scale should be subject to local democratic control and those who envisage local government as essentially 'local' and concerned more with the efficient and accountable delivery of services than with 'strategic' policy issues. Those who favour the first definition will advocate an improvement in the present two-tier arrangements; those who prefer the more local definition will favour a simple one-tier or unitary structure. This divide by no means runs along party lines.

Some studies have suggested that there are at least 13 different structures for metropolitan government to be found across the world. But it will be enough to consider only seven that have been suggested specifically for London. (Some of these could of course be easily adapted to the metropolitan county areas.)

Unitary models

Some academics and political commentators looking at the far-from-glorious history of the GLC believe that the Herbert Commission made a mistake in opting for a two-tier system of government in London. It was understandable, however, in the light of expert opinion in the late fifties when the problems of an expanding conurbation and 'overheating' in the London economy seemed to demand a broad sweep planning approach. In the changed circumstances of the eighties these factors no longer seem to have the same importance and certainly cannot now justify the confusing and counter-democratic division of responsibility between two councils in every part of the capital. But if a one-tier or 'unitary' system is to be introduced it has to be effective, and able to operate without recourse to poorly accountable joint boards and unaccountable quangos. This points towards the creation of larger unitary bodies than the present London boroughs which were never designed to do the job.

Model 1: The five large boroughs scheme
One cogent unitary scheme has been floated by Dr Ken Young of the Policy Studies Institute, historian both of metropolitan government and of the fiasco of the GLC housing strategy. Dr Young argues that five units, each with a population about the size of Birmingham's, should be carved out of the present GLC area.

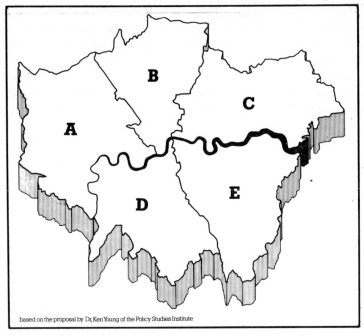

based on the proposal by Dr, Ken Young of the Policy Studies Institute

THE 'FIVE BIG BOROUGHS' SOLUTION

Dividing up the capital in this way would create financially viable units that would overcome some of the present anomalies in the financial resources of each borough. (For instance, the City of Westminster, the richest of the present 32 boroughs, has a ratable value ten times greater than that of Lewisham.) Under the Young scheme each of the five new units would combine both rich and poor districts and would enormously reduce the elaborate 'equalization' calculations that the Department of the Environment has to make before allocating grants. This would reduce civil service man hours and could lead to less government interference.

Such well-resourced units of governments could bring together all the local government services under a single roof and would represent an enormous simplification of the proposed Thatcher scheme. The new 'superboroughs' would not only take over all the present borough services but could add education in the inner London districts (the ILEA would go), could assume responsibility for refuse disposal as well as refuse collection, for the fire service, for grants to voluntary organizations, for both structure planning and local plans, and for all but the major highways.

Because each of the five new units would contain parts of both inner and outer London, Dr Young envisages a more effective strategy to rehabilitate the run-down inner-city areas and a more rational approach to rehousing policy. Because of the social mix within the boundaries of each new council it is unlikely that any of these new boroughs would fall under continuous one-party control – a real gain, Dr Young argues, for local democracy.

Nevertheless, the shortcomings of the scheme are obvious. Although joint boards and quangos may not be necessary, some kind of joint cooperation between the councils would continue to be essential, especially on planning. There is a question mark too over how acceptable the boundaries might be: although Dr Young thinks there is some degree of continuity with the old county divisions they look highly artificial, especially in relation to the central London area. Clearly they could not serve as real 'strategic' authorities in terms of public transport, water supply and sewerage. Londoners would continue to pay separate rate charges to unaccountable bodies.

But, most fundamentally, the structure fails to deliver a 'voice for London' in a form likely to be acceptable to parliamentary critics of the present Thatcher proposals. Dr Young suggests that the five mayors could work together as an effective lobby, but there is no guarantee that they could speak with a united voice.

Model 2: The LCC resurrected

A second unitary model which seems to meet the requirements of those who want to keep a 'voice for London' has been put forward by George Jones, LSE Professor of Government and, quite separately, by Tyrell Burgess and Tony Travers of the North East London Polytechnic.

George Jones is co-biographer of Herbert Morrison and an admirer of what he achieved as leader of the old London County Council. But his proposal, which amounts to resurrecting the

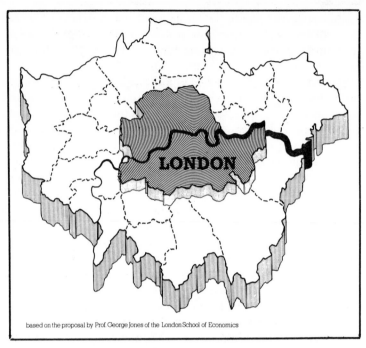

based on the proposal by Prof. George Jones of the London School of Economics

LCC RESURRECTED:
outer boundaries to be reviewed.

LCC in a modified form, is not based on a sentimental attachment to the 'good old days' at County Hall. Ever since 1889 many people have argued that the LCC area is just too big to be genuinely local. George Jones argues that this is no longer the case. The population of the 12 inner London boroughs and the City of London is now just two and a quarter million, no longer huge by world standards.

His solution is to create a new all-purpose authority from what has become the inner-city core of London. Professor Jones argues that the old LCC area still survives in many people's minds as the real London: people who live within its borders have a sense of being 'Londoners' in a way that will never be possible for many of those who inhabit the suburbs. This could give the proposed authority a head start in winning acceptance by the public.

But not only would the area form a 'natural' unit, it would also preserve the Inner London Education Authority as an administrative unit (avoiding the bureaucratic disruption implied in the Young Plan) at the same time as bringing it into the direct democratic control of a council that would also have responsibility for the newly integrated and closely related housing and social services departments. The new 'LCC' would run fire and refuse services and provide a planning authority that could deal cogently with the problems of the central business zone (which under the present arrangement is divided among at least five separate boroughs). It would be the equivalent of the Paris City Council, which is responsible only for the central historic core of the Paris conurbation.

Indeed, if the Jones plan is ever carried through, the 'City of London' would in effect extend its boundary outwards and become at last a part of the democratic structure of London local government with the Lord Mayor (assuming the title is retained) as the symbolic head of the capital.

As with the proposals put forward by Ken Young, this new local authority would have the advantage of combining rich borough with poor to create a very healthy rate base. (The City of London has an enormous rateable value exceeding that of the whole of Wales.) As a result the present equalization arrangements (as with Model 1) could be greatly simplified. Again, these resources, combined in one all-embracing planning authority, could be applied to tackle the rehabilitation of down-at-heel inner-city areas. This could be supplemented by a council-led and coordinated employment strategy aimed at reversing the long-standing economic decline of these areas.

The Burgess-Travers version of this new model of London government elaborates by suggesting the re-creation of parish councils to cater for very local community needs. It is also more specific in treating the question of what should become of the present outer London zone. Some of the outer boroughs – such as Croydon, which has a population of over 300,000 – could be made into unitary councils as they stand. Other boundaries, Burgess and Travers suggest, would have to be redrawn to create bigger units – one of these might even be a reconstituted

Middlesex. But questions like these should be decided on only after an inquiry.

The pattern of a unitary LCC, surrounded by fewer but more powerful boroughs, therefore emerges. Where cooperation between these is necessary, Burgess and Travers suggest it should be through voluntary committees. No joint boards or quangos would be needed.

This proposal is obviously worthy of serious consideration as it apparently offers neat answers to some of the most enduring problems of governing the capital. It offers simple one-tier government; it provides for some local identity; it allays the fears of the suburbs; it offers some relief from the need for excessive equalization; it achieves a 'voice for London'. It does, however, present a practical political problem: the Labour Party at present holds a large majority of the seats in the inner London boroughs. It would seem highly likely, short of a big collapse in the Labour vote, that – like the old LCC – the new one would be more or less constantly under its control. It might therefore be very difficult for a Conservative government to adopt this radical plan. In any case it could never satisfy those who would like to see metropolitan transport, metropolitan road strategy, 'green-belt' preservation, water supply and sewerage, and all such important London-wide issues under local democratic control.

The only way to achieve that degree of democratic accountability while retaining the unitary principle would be to create one single giant council for the whole of Greater London. While this idea would have won the warm support of H. G. Wells, it really is a political non-starter in the 1980s. Those who want to see a directly elected metropolitan government have had to accept the need for a two-tier structure.

Regional models

The supporters of a two-tier structure have solid ground upon which to rest their case: both the Herbert Commission that led to the establishment of the GLC, and the Redcliffe-Maud Commission on Local Government in England (report published in 1969) considered such an arrangement unavoidable in a larger conurbation.* But that leaves enormous scope for disagreement about what powers each tier should have and about where boundaries should be drawn. In the present debate at least four models have been suggested.

Model 3: A London assembly

Not all Conservatives in London have been bowled over by the present GLC abolition plans, least of all the Conservative councillors who actually sit at County Hall. The decision to wind up the all-London council fell like a bombshell on the 41-strong Conservative Group. With a shrewd if occasionally flippant new leader in Alan Greengross, the County Hall Tories had been relishing the prospect of turning out an unpopular Ken Livingstone and his Labour administration at the next GLC elections, due in 1985. Without any consultation having taken place between them and the national Conservative leadership, they found that they were on a countdown to political oblivion.

The reaction of the Tories at County Hall was to launch a plan which went as far as it could to meet Mrs Thatcher's objections to the GLC while at the same time retaining the principle of an elected London-wide council. In its final form – issued in populist shape, cartoons and all, in a pamphlet entitled *Getting It Together For London* – the plan proposed that, on abolition of the GLC, a new elected body should be set up to take its place. But the scheme put forward by the GLC Tories aims to preserve the upper tier of a two-tier structure in a minimalist form.

Under their plan the GLC would be abolished and replaced by an 'assembly' that would not in law be a local authority at all but 'a new type of body with its specific functions conferred upon it by legislation'. It represents an attempt to stop such an assembly ever becoming a 'son of Frankenstein', as Mrs Thatcher had initially dubbed the whole idea. This new body would not have the GLC's power to spend ratepayers' money in controversial ways. Any spending other than on the specified

---

* Redcliffe-Maud favoured 'unitary' local government for the whole of England *except* the metropolitan areas. It is an irony that the present Thatcher plan would produce 'unitary' councils *only* in the metropolitan areas.

functions would be illegal. To be doubly certain, the plan provides for its annual budget to be subject to the approval of the Secretary of State himself. Such an arrangement would ensure that this new body would not be 'wasteful', one of the chief charges laid at the GLC's door.

The County Hall Conservatives also bent over backwards to stress that everything at present done by the GLC that could conceivably be done by the boroughs should be passed to them. The new assembly would be a 'slim-line' authority with a very small staff carrying out only 'framework' functions. This was envisaged as laying out 'working parameters' to guide the boroughs on planning matters (the detailed planning work presently done at County Hall would go), running a small department to take charge of the GLC Debt and the GLC Pension Fund, allocating grants to voluntary bodies, and administrating the London rate equalization scheme.

It would also continue to be responsible for the all-London services of fire and waste disposal: where possible such services could either be privatized or delegated to the boroughs for day-to-day running, the latter option – it was stressed – being fully in line with the Tory Party manifesto pledge to pass the GLC functions to the boroughs wherever practicable.

The great advantage offered by the arrangement, the GLC Tories claim, is that there would be no need for any joint boards or quangos. All the remaining GLC services would be under the control of one single body that would be able to decide priorities of spending between one service and another, so adding greater efficiency to better democratic accountability. The solution also offers a continuing 'voice for London' although, one would suspect, considerably muted by the narrowness of its remit.

However, this particular variation on the existing two-tier model presents practical problems. If it is to be severely restricted in its scope it would be very difficult to convince the public that it is really important enough to justify going out to vote in an election (and if the poll fell to less than, say, 30 per cent this would seriously undermine any claim it might have to speak for Londoners). Secondly, an assembly with such little power and so little to do might find it difficult to attract good-quality candidates or able administrators.

Nevertheless, it could find surprising support in the House of Lords because it claims to deliver 95 per cent of the Tory election manifesto pledge: peers may not feel that voting for this scheme offends against the principle that manifesto commitments are sacrosanct.

Model 4: The Copenhagen solution

At the heart of the GLC Tory policy lies the notion that it should be possible to have a 'strategic' upper-tier authority that makes important planning decisions for the capital, without a huge bureaucracy and without major service functions. There are examples of such authorities elsewhere that seem to work.

Alan Norton, of the Institute of Local Government Studies in Birmingham, has completed a useful survey of metropolitan governments in both Europe and North America. Many of these operate in a local government structure unlike anything known in Britain (in Europe the basic units of local government tend to be much smaller than in the UK). This means that lessons drawn from experience abroad have to be applied with caution here. Nevertheless, the approach used by the Danes to tackle the problems of the Copenhagen metropolitan area seems to offer a useful example of small, 'strategic' upper-tier authorities working well. It could be seen as an alternative to the present GLC Conservatives' scheme.

Greater Copenhagen covers an area of some 1,000 square miles and includes two cities and three counties with a total population of nearly two million. In the early seventies, for much the same reasons as in Greater London, it was decided to establish an upper-tier authority to coordinate and plan for the whole conurbation. The Greater Copenhagen Council first met in 1974 and had 'strategic' powers in relation to planning, public transport, water supply, environmental pollution and the hospital service.

Its achievements seem impressive. It has successfully drafted the overall plan (a plan that the lower-tier bodies have to adhere to) and won major improvements in public transport: the council has introduced zonal fares, common bus and rail tickets, and has assumed responsibility for the region's rail services. The number of people travelling by bus rose by a third in its first eight years of operation. In its role of hospital planner it effectively controls over half of all the public expenditure in Greater Copenhagen.

It therefore comes as a considerable surprise to learn that the Greater Copenhagen council had a staff of only 114 in 1983. (The GLC has 21,000 employees on its books.) This seems to conform to the GLC Conservative dream of government without bureaucracy. Even more surprising is the fact that the council is not directly elected. Its members are chosen from among councillors sitting on the city and county authorities and from other smaller municipalities. In England this is generally considered to be a sure formula for a council composed of 'political nobodies' (perhaps unenthusiastic volunteers who can spare the time) and for poor accountability to the electors. What the Copenhagen experience seems to show is that the first assumption at least need not be true, when the body carries both power and prestige.

Public interest in the council, however, does not seem to be great. And Alan Norton points to a broad social democratic consensus among the constitutent authorities. However, the idea may merit further examination.

Model 5: A Strathclyde solution

Elsewhere in Europe metropolitan problems have been approached rather differently. Directly elected upper-tier authorities are to be found both in Holland and in Germany but covering a wider area than just the large cities themselves. Rijnmond (Rhine estuary), for instance, takes in not just Rotterdam but 15 other municipalities on either side of the Rhine. Such an approach applied to London would mean substantially redrawing the boundaries of the GLC to make it a better unit for planning and controlling services.

It is not necessary, however, to use foreign examples to show how this approach could work. Since 1975 a similar local government structure has been in operation in Scotland.

North of the Border the reform of local government has been carried through quite independently of England along lines suggested by a Royal Commission under Lord Wheatley in

Strathclyde Region, an amalgamation of Glasgow and six counties, has proved an effective planning unit for West Scotland.

1969. Wheatley was very influenced by two arguments: firstly that the boundaries of local authorities should be drawn to maximize their ability to carry out their functions both efficiently and democratically. This implied large authorities for certain services and smaller ones for others, creating the inescapable need for a two-tier system. This approval echoes the conclusions of the Herbert Commission. (But Wheatley had more freedom than Herbert in the question of drawing boundaries; Herbert's remit was to look only at the metropolitan built-up area.)

Wheatley found a second argument, that the traditional split between town and country made no sense in a modern and mobile society (the Redcliffe-Maud Commission also reached a similar conclusion). The concept of a city/region which could cover a wide area delineated by travelling patterns, either to work, to go shopping or to enjoy recreation in the countryside, was chosen by Wheatley to be the foundation of a logical local government structure.

The Wheatley report was implemented with a few minor changes in the 1973 Local Government (Scotland) Act. Scotland was divided into nine regions based on 'travel-to-work' patterns. The largest of these, the Strathclyde Region, was centred on Glasgow but took in much of Western Scotland. It had a population of two and a half million (about half of the Scottish population) and absorbed not only Glasgow but its five surrounding counties.

Strathclyde took over from these old authorities in 1975. As the upper-tier authority it was given responsibility for nearly all the important council services (in sharp contrast to the GLC). As well as transport and main roads, structure (or 'strategic') planning, regional parks and economic development (all at one time or another a GLC responsibility) it had control of schools and further education; it was to provide a wide range of social services; and it ran the region's water supply. (Wheatley suggested that housing, too, should be a regional function, but this was given to the lower-tier district authorities.) Strathclyde, like all the new Scottish regional councils, was clearly to be the major local government unit for people living within its borders. The Districts, including one for the City of Glasgow, were now to be mainly housing authorities with responsibility elsewhere limited to minor local services such as parks and libraries, refuse collection and street cleaning, and some local planning powers (strictly subordinate to the regional plan). Symbolic of the power relationship between region and district the bills for rates were issued by the top-tier authority not, as they are in London, by the lower-tier bodies.

Despite the economic climate it has had to work in, the achievements of Strathclyde have been in stark contrast to the relative failure of the GLC.

Before 1975 both water supply and transport had passed into the hands of joint boards, a sure indication that the old local council structure was finding it difficult to cope. Under the new system water services passed back under direct democratic control and could now be planned for and developed on a regional scale: the old arrangement whereby every town had its own, often inadequate, reservoir could now give way to new larger-scale works that kept pace with rising consumer demand.

In the case of public transport, however, the impact of the new regional council has been even more greatly felt. The Glasgow Underground system has been modernized and linked to the British Rail network: derelict rail tunnels running under the busiest parts of Glasgow have been reopened to modern electric British Rail trains, and now work has begun on the electrification of the important Ayr–Glasgow commuter railway. All this has been done largely at council expense. Strathclyde has revolutionized both rail and bus services through its power to dictate the level of fares, the level of service and the co-ordination of timetables. This has, of course, involved a subsidy from the ratepayers running, in 1984, at £50 million. In return for this contribution from the public purse even British Rail trains are now painted in Strathclyde's own livery, an unmistakable bright orange-red.

Under this Scottish two-tier system the district councils are certainly the poor relations and some, like Glasgow, have found the role difficult to accept. But conflict between the two tiers has never approached the levels found in London. Friction has been kept to a minimum, partly due to the predominantly Labour control of both upper- and lower-tier councils. However, that is not the whole story. A government committee under Sir Anthony Stodart reviewed the workings of the system in 1981 and reduced some possible areas of complaint by largely removing duplication of function. It is also quite likely that the strength of the upper-tier compared with lower-tier councils has made some contribution.

To apply anything approaching a Strathclyde solution in the London area would mean redrawing the boundaries of local authorities to reflect 'travel-to-work' patterns. Some planners have suggested extending the border to include the M25 and the metropolitan green belt. Others suggest going even further to create a genuine London region that would include the important commuter towns that are beyond the green belt. Such an authority could be given powers at present in the hands of central government (for example the running of the health service) and others that belong to non-elected bodies such as

London Regional Transport, British Rail and Thames Water Authority. It might assume some responsibility for economic, industrial and employment policy for the region as a whole.

Of course such a policy is unlikely to appeal to free-market Conservatives whose aim is to reduce the work and the power of local government to a minimum. Even for those who see social and economic planning as a legitimate role for local government action there remains the question of how practical a very large authority with a population of some 12 million people might be. It certainly would offer a formidable power base that could challenge central government at times. For those on the left the prospects of ever gaining a majority on such a council would be slight, and that might be considered another unacceptable feature. But it could have strong appeal to members of the Alliance parties who are committed to decentralization of Westminster power and to a system of proportional representation that would almost certainly preclude one-party control.

In the short term, though, the plan faces a major practical difficulty: it could reasonably be introduced only as a reform of the whole English local government system because of the radical boundary changes that would be required.

Model 7: A stronger GLC?

There is, however, another possible and quite radical reform of the present GLC (and, conceivably, of the metropolitan county councils) that could be carried through along similar lines to the Scottish system without any boundary alterations. This scheme would increase the power of the upper-tier council to allow it to operate more effectively as a custodian of the wider metropolitan interests, much as originally envisaged by the Herbert Commission. It has the advantage of having already been subject to a detailed inquiry conducted by a senior figure in the Conservative Party only a few years ago.

In 1977 Horace Cutler had led the Tories to victory in the GLC elections amid growing criticism of the County Hall machine, criticism which came as much from the Labour Party as from within the ranks of London's Conservatives. In order to guard his political flanks Mr (later Sir Horace) Cutler launched the idea of a thorough review of the workings of London local government. This led to the establishment of a high-powered inquiry led by a respected veteran of Conservative local politics, Sir Frank Marshall. Now, as Lord Marshall, he is Vice-Chairman of the Conservative Party.

A down-to-earth northerner, Frank Marshall had served as leader of the Leeds City Council and was perfectly familiar with metropolitan problems. He approached his new task of reviewing the government of the capital with characteristic thoroughness, setting up a team of advisers that included three professors, several management consultants, and one former government minister, Sir Christopher Chataway. The inquiry took evidence from hundreds of people and organizations with a special interest in London affairs and with ideas on what County Hall's role should be.

The Marshall Report, published in 1978, was generally welcomed as a model of its kind, well researched and crystal-clear in its conclusions. Marshall had started with the assumption that

A metropolitan authority is necessary to enable London government to function properly. The total interest of London as a whole transcends that of its constituent parts, their local needs and individual aspirations. It must be cared for by a corporate body charged with taking an overall view of issues and events in Metropolitan terms.

Given this assumption, Marshall concluded that the GLC must be transformed into an effective 'strategic' council for the capital: that meant both divesting itself of tasks that could be better run by the boroughs and strengthening its powers so that it could act as 'the recognized guardian of the interests of the community as a whole'. To the extent the Marshall policy aimed to create an all-London council with a minimum of bureaucracy but with very substantial teeth.

He recommended that all detailed planning matters should go to the boroughs and that, where possible, the borough councils should act as agents to carry out GLC work. But, if the system was to work well and if the credibility of the GLC was to be restored, County Hall had to be seen to make the strategic decisions for London and, more importantly, have the power to see them carried out.

Lord Marshall then sketched out a detailed blueprint of how this should be done. He wanted stronger planning powers for County Hall: local plans should not be allowed to vary from the overall GLC London plan. As far as transport was concerned County Hall should assume full responsibility for the complete public transport network in London, with power to set fares on London Transport and even to control the suburban railway services by means of a 'contract with British Rail'.

In line with the changed economic circumstances of the late seventies Lord Marshall also wanted the GLC to be given a leading role in attracting new jobs to London and in the planning and location of industrial estates. The derelict acres of Docklands were seen as playing an important part in any jobs strategy and Lord Marshall wanted to pass responsibility for redeveloping them entirely to County Hall, removing any borough involvement which many critics believed had held up progress.

However, Lord Marshall wanted to go beyond simply increasing the power of the GLC at the expense of the boroughs. It could become effective only if it also took powers from Whitehall. He wanted to see trunk roads (at present in the hands of the Department of Transport) pass into GLC control. He wanted the Department of the Environment to hand over the power it had to allocate resources for housing development in the boroughs. Most controversially of all, he suggested that the DoE should continue to decide on the total rate support to be paid to London but that the GLC should decide how to distribute it to the individual boroughs. This would mean taking real power away from the civil servants and putting it in the hands of London's elected representatives.

For the future, Lord Marshall looked forward to a strengthening of local government in London by setting up a GLC Police Committee which would approve the police budget and have a say in the appointment of the Metropolitan Police Commissioner. And, casting his eyes back to the days of the LCC, he envisaged responsibility for controlling London's health services passing back to County Hall, which would oversee the work of the capital's health authorities.

Ironically, some of those who now fight to preserve and strengthen the GLC, like Ken Livingstone, attacked the

Marshall Report at the time as being too 'academic'. Even more ironically, both Patrick Jenkin and Kenneth Baker gave evidence to the inquiry in favour of a stronger GLC and may have helped shape Lord Marshall's final conclusions.

The Report's recommendations have never been implemented. To the borough leaders they were too reminiscent of the 'Big Brother' attitude of the GLC that Horace Cutler had once denounced. Any attempt to revive the scheme now would be certain to run into opposition from this quarter. Again, the chances of getting proposals along these lines through parliament have not been increased by the present government's unwillingness to devolve power from Whitehall. In addition, the revamping of Rate Support Grant along the lines suggested by the Marshall Report would mean an almost certainly complex reform of local government finance across the country. For these reasons a Marshall-type solution to the crisis in London government seems an unlikely, if intriguing, possibility.

Which way forward?

Despite these alternatives on offer it seems likely that the majority of Tory MPs will prefer to stick with the government's present plans. But the unitary models might look an attractive alternative, offering as they do clear gains in accountability. Some changes in the present two-tier structure to make it more effective cannot, however, be ruled out as a possibility should parliament decide to set up a new inquiry into London government.

There remains a chance that government anxiety to secure maximum support for its present policy may lead it to suggest marginal change in the present plan, to ward off the criticism that it has not provided for a 'voice for London'. It could suggest the setting up of a special parliamentary committee of London MPs to maintain a close watch over London affairs. This idea was floated by Patrick Jenkin in the autumn of 1984 and received a scornful reception. There was the obvious political point that the GLC is Labour-controlled while a majority of London MPs are Conservative. But more seriously it was feared that a lack of any real power for such a committee would turn it into a mere 'talking shop'. The nearest equivalent seems to be the Scottish Grand Committee, which has embarrassingly little prestige in parliament. This suggestion does, therefore, appear to be unlikely to reach the parliamentary starting post.

However, the history of London government has been full of unexpected twists and turns that add fascination to any speculation about the future. We are now going to take a look at the immediate prospects.

10. THE FUTURE

One of the supreme ironies ... will be in the Secretary of State's [Patrick Jenkin's] own constituency. It appears that a GLC golf course will be divided so that nine holes will be in Redbridge, eight in Havering, and one in Epping Forest. It is rumoured that Conservative members are only concerned about the destination of the nineteenth hole. (Dr John Cunningham, opposition Environment spokesman, 3 December 1984)

Thus far, we have considered what has happened and why. But what is to become of London? Although the alternatives considered in the previous chapter have not so far been on the government's agenda they are far from academic. It is now more than conceivable that sooner or later some will have to be given serious attention as options.

The government was always going to have a rough ride with a Bill of this nature, but few doubted until late in 1984 that it would actually get its way in the end. Since then, however, the outcome has become ever more uncertain.

The government's aim was to abolish the GLC and metropolitan counties at midnight on 31 March 1986. To meet that target the Bill would be needed on the Statute Book by November 1985 at the very latest. Officials had made plain from the start that even if there were no hitches and no opposition this would be a very close-run thing. Of the many possible pitfalls they identified two that could be ruinous unless they were avoided at the drafting stage.

The first was the problem of hybridity. This occurs when a Bill affects both public and private interests or when a Bill is seen to be treating similar bodies in different ways.

If a Bill is deemed hybrid it passes through parliament in a different way, the key feature being that it is endlessly time-consuming – which would be the kiss of death for this particular piece of legislation. A hybrid Bill passes to a special select committee of the House of Commons for detailed scrutiny during which evidence can be called and taken from external parties.

Anxiety about hybridity led to all mention of the controversial Greater London Enterprise Board being excluded from the Bill. This is because although GLEB was set up by the GLC with GLC funds it operates as a separate commercial entity.

Nevertheless, counsel informed the Bill's opponents on the morning of the first day of the second reading debate – Monday 3 December – that there was a prima-facie case of potential hybridity affecting clauses 24 and 39 of the Bill, which deal with the Northumbria Police Authority and local authority airports.

The Speaker said he had been through the Bill 'with the

greatest care to consider the possibility of hybridity' (implying that he did not think it was hybrid) but he did not preclude further action by the House.

The second potential problem identified by officials was the constitutional issues which would arise if such a controversial proposal as abolition of democratic councils was to be dealt with in an 'enabling' Bill devoid of detail but full of powers for the Secretary of State to do as he saw fit as and when detailed work was completed.

At one stage such a Bill was a real possibility because the pressure of time and solid non-cooperation by the councils involved made a detailed Bill appear out of the question. However, in the event, enough time and detail was available to incorporate some concrete proposals into the Bill before its publication on 22 November 1984. There was not enough detail, however (and certainly not enough confidence on the government's part) for reserve powers to be omitted altogether. The Bill is most curious (and exceptionally poorly drafted) therefore, in that it purports to be a Bill of detail yet it includes some 60 reserve powers for the Secretary of State – some of which could come to grief in the House of Lords, which tends not to smile kindly on such behaviour.

But at least the government had escaped being forced to accept the entire Bill as a major constitutional issue, which would have meant taking the entire committee stage on the floor of the Commons, creating havoc in the business of the House, possibly for weeks.

The second reading

The Bill had its second reading in the House of Commons on 3 and 4 December. Patrick Jenkin opened the debate with a spectacularly poor speech during which he was repeatedly attacked – 'savaged' was the word used by some of his own advisers – by his own side.

Dr John Cunningham, for the opposition, reminded the government that Kenneth Baker, Local Government Minister charged with trying to get the legislation on the Statute Book,

WHAT THE PAPERS SAID ABOUT ABOLITION AND THE GLC

BEYOND OUR KEN

... The government needs to go back to the drawing board. There is a good case for ending the metropolitan county tier of government and devolving more powers to the districts. But the government has yet to discover it, or work out how to implement it wisely. And it is a mistake to include London in such a reform: the evidence from Paris, and even New York these days, is that international cities need strong city-wide government.

Urban government in Britain is a mess. It allows extremist caucuses (usually Labour) to take control. It then tries to curb their lunacies with undemocratic Whitehall controls (usually Tory). As a result town halls and Whitehall blame each other for exercising power without responsibility, and the electorate is short-changed. Other countries manage better.

Sunday Times, 1.7.84

PHONEY

Much-troubled Mr Patrick Jenkin is according to reports, about to offer London a new mini-Parliament to replace the Greater London Council once the Environment Secretary finally does away with it in 1986. The plan is for a special committee of all the London MPs, perhaps together with a beefed-up role for the London Boroughs Association.

The idea is not new ... But we hope that Mr Jenkin will leave it well alone.

It is understandable that, confronted with a mountain of evidence that their present plans are a hugely unpopular mess, ministers and officials should be looking for some compromise as a way out. But the compromise has to be genuine. The message from right across the political spectrum is that after the GLC goes there will still be a number of services which ought to be run London-wide; that these will still need money; and that money can only properly be raised by an elected, London-wide authority. Nothing less will do.

Standard, 17.9.84

WHAT COMES AFTER THE GLC?

... On balance, however, the judgement that the GLC comprises neither the right structure nor the right mix of powers and responsibilities to govern London effectively seems to be sound.

The Government's solution, seemingly based more in party

political advantage than in studied improvement of the capital's administration, is unsound.... The principle of unitary local government where it can be created without loss of efficiency or accountability is a desirable general objective. But London is different. It is both a collection of villages and small towns strung together by in-fill development and traffic jams *and* a cohesive capital city of international importance. The boroughs cater for the first; a city-wide authority – directly elected, with independent taxation revenues and powers to match its functions and status – is required for the second.

Financial Times, 20.9.84

VOTE FOR – WHAT?

No impediment now stands in the way of abolishing the GLC. It was always reasonable to get rid of this trifling, but expensive, subordinate tier of local government. It could be used for little, but was a perfect instrument for cynical exploitation and abuse. The pity is that the Minister concerned, Mr Jenkin, an intelligent, principled and decent man, handled the case of the transitional year ineptly.

But 'inept' does not mean 'wrong'. Local government generally is in declining repute. The Metropolitan Counties, so fatuously created by Mr Peter Walker 10 years ago, are nowhere held in respect. ... One devoutly hopes that the Minister will now come out fighting. Getting rid of the GLC is something to be proud of.

Daily Telegraph, 22.9.84

THE REFORM OF LOCAL COUNCILS

... Opposition to the abolition proposals implies neither support for the more far-fetched antics of Mr Ken Livingstone at the GLC nor a belief that the present structure for urban (or shire) local government is satisfactory.

But there are certain criteria which must be fulfilled for changes to be acceptable.

Arrangements

The first is that the new arrangements stand a reasonable chance of being an improvement on the old. The second is that accountability is not reduced, so that pressure for efficiency and sensitivity to local aspirations is not diminished. The third is that democracy and democratic principles are neither weakened nor violated.

The Bill fails on all three counts. If the view that political malice is behind the Bill is to be discounted, the proposals have to be judged as an attempt to improve the system of devolved government by moving towards unitary multi-service authorities.

But by decreeing the end without giving any thought to the means the Government has produced proposals which move backwards from the concept of unitary councils.

... The three key areas requiring amendment are the Government's reserve powers, joint boards and London. The Bill is littered with reserve powers to give a degree of centralized control over local issues which makes efficient service provision less, rather than more, likely.

Conundrum

... London is a conundrum. At least in the metropolitan areas the major cities such as Leeds, Liverpool, Manchester, will still have a city-wide authority after abolition. The capital will not. The Government has had no answer to critics who point out the absurdity of ignoring the common interests which exist between the disparate villages and communities which make up one of the world's largest and most important capitals. The case for abolishing the Greater London Council is clearly much weaker than for the metropolitan counties and, on present evidence, ought not to proceed at all.

Financial Times, 12.12.84

THE ENTITY OF LONDON

Whatever happens to administration, the Government cannot abolish London. Between Richmond and Hammersmith there are shared concerns (for example, the flight path into Heathrow!). Denizens of the 32 boroughs share interests in transport, public safety and public health; there is an emotion and a culture that is London, which ought to be expressed through a political organ more local than parliament yet less parochial than the borough.

... Blueprints for a directly-elected London-wide body abound.

... A GLC Mark II, ministers have exclaimed when offered such amendments. It certainly need not, and should not, be that. The experience of GLC Mark I has given enough ammunition to redefine more tightly the new body's role, protecting the citizens of London from bad spending, overmanning and political manipulation.

London's administration has always shown an untidy pattern in which the only consistent element has been the intense interest of Whitehall, and not only in public order. There is no reason why a reconstructed London-wide body should fit into any of the existing categories, with wide general powers to tax and spend; it would in any case be required to enter a close and continuing fiscal relationship with Whitehall. The government of the capital will always be anomalous. The passage of the abolition bill presents the opportunity not to remove the anomaly but to establish the necessary London-wide element on the sure footing of a direct franchise.

Times, 27.12.84

had been the joint author of a pamphlet, *Maybe it's because we're Londoners*, in which he wrote: 'The strategic role of the GLC should be enhanced ... Far from the GLC being allowed greater independence Whitehall has, quite wrongly, interfered more and more ... The GLC must become a proper strategic authority.'

Remarkably similar views in support of the GLC had been put by Patrick Jenkin to the Marshall inquiry into London government.

Tory backbenchers followed one another to warn the government about one aspect of the Bill or another – Eldon Griffiths complained about the potential for disruption of what were currently very satisfactory and efficient policing arrangements in the metropolitan counties, Sir Philip Goodhart was one of many to urge the government not to leave London without a 'voice'.

Tory dissent peaked on the second day – Tuesday 4 December – when Edward Heath rose to speak at 4.37 p.m. He made an 18-minute speech which was widely regarded as one of his best performances since he was prime minister in 1974. It was sharp, witty and to the point.

He warned that the Bill was in for a rough ride:

I have one word of advice for my right honourable friend the Secretary of State for the Environment which I hope he will find helpful. If those in another place [the House of Lords] throw out the Bill, he will not be able to do anything; but if they amend it he should be ready with a plan for the overall government of London together with the rest of the Bill. I give him that simple and straightforward advice.

Cheered by the opposition and raising chortles from many of his own side including Kenneth Baker, Local Government Minister, but not including Nicholas Ridley, the hapless Transport Secretary, whose contribution to the debate Mr Heath described as 'a pathetic image of a speech', nor a stony-faced Patrick Jenkin, the former Tory premier warmed to his theme.

He was dismissive of Sir Philip Goodhart's idea for a powerless talking shop of London MPs to watch over the capital's affairs:

Let the Government not come forward with the idea that the House of Commons should have a London Committee. We all know that that is not to the point. Such a committee would not have been democratically elected for London. Furthermore, such a committee could be altered. We all know that the Scottish Grand Committee has often been adjusted by various Governments to suit their own purposes. We need an overall elected body for London and, I believe, for the metropolitan counties.

In a passage of his speech which could turn out to have been pointedly prophetic, with the Lords in mind, Mr Heath urged Mr Jenkin to think ahead

to the point at which he will be forced to have an overall London authority, which will then be a reformed one ... In local authority matters one should always, above all, move slowly and cautiously. I am afraid that that is what the Government have failed to recognize on this occasion. Accordingly, I ask my right honourable friend to think ahead to the stage at which he will be required to provide an overall authority for the greatest capital in the world and for the metropolitan boroughs.

The government got its second reading with a majority of 132, but the whips were anxious about the tone of the debate from the Tory side.

The committee

Still, the government had nothing to offer its opponents when the Bill reappeared in the Commons on Wednesday 12 December. The Bill came into the Commons because the government had agreed, as part of its anxiety to defuse any constitutional complaints, to take the committee stage of Clause 1, the key abolition proposals, on the floor of the full House.

The opposition moved an amendment which would have prevented abolition until after a Royal Commission had reported on local government in Greater London and the metropolitan counties. Several other amendments, taken with the principal one, proposed alternative sorts of inquiry, but all in the same spirit. They fell by majorities of around 50.

But at the end of the two-day debate, at 12.37 a.m. on Friday

14 December, the government's majority collapsed to one of its lowest levels since 1979 and certainly its lowest since the 1983 election.

The humiliation occurred on an amendment moved by a Tory, Patrick Cormack, that the GLC

shall be replaced by a directly elected authority representing the area presently administered by the Greater London Council, such authority's functions and powers to be determined by Parliament following an inquiry by a select committee of the House of Commons into the functions and powers of the Greater London Council.

The government's majority was just 23. There had been a two-line rather than draconian three-line whip on the vote, arguably to allow MPs to abstain by staying away from the House rather than embarrass the government by marching into the opposition lobbies or staying glued to their Commons benches in large numbers. But nobody had expected the government to lose more than 100 of its own MPs.

As if this was not bad enough for increasingly anxious government whips, it was all happening at a time when the Tory leadership seemed to be drifting out of touch with its own MPs on a wide range of issues – mass revolt by Tory backbenchers forced a U-turn by Sir Keith Joseph on plans to cut student grants, Patrick Jenkin was howled down when he acted as errand boy to bring the House news of the Treasury's decision to cut £600m out of housing capital expenditure, Nicholas Ridley had to bring consideration of his Civil Aviation Bill to a stop in committee because Tory MPs opposed to Stansted as the third London Airport were making progress impossible.

This was not just bored MPs at play because the prime minister was out of the country (visiting China and the US). It was the long-awaited eruption of dissent caused principally by a growing unwillingness by Cabinet ministers to listen to and consult the only people who can help them implement their policy – their own backbenchers.

In the Lords, too, signs of government nervousness appeared with, for example, the seemingly petulant decision to withdraw the Tory Whip from Lord Alport, Minister of State for Commonwealth Relations from 1959 to 1961, who had voted

WHO PATRICK JENKIN PLANS TO PUT IN THE PLACE OF LONDON'S DEMOCRATICALLY ELECTED COUNCILLORS.

HEAD OF EDUCATION.

HEAD OF PLANNING.

HEAD OF TRAFFIC CONTROL.

HEAD OF FIRE SERVICE.

HEAD OF HOUSING IMPROVEMENTS.

HEAD OF ARTS.

HEAD OF WASTE DISPOSAL.

HEAD OF GRANTS TO VOLUNTARY GROUPS.

HEAD OF FLOODING AND LAND DRAINAGE.

In the Abolition Bill, Patrick Jenkin states quite clearly who he's appointing to run London if the GLC goes.

Himself.

The Bill gives him direct control over all the Whitehall committees and joint boards which would take over the majority of the GLC's functions.

A free hand to do whatever he wants to do whether anyone else likes it or not.

And that's not all. It also gives him the power to change the actual details of the Bill itself after it's been approved by the Houses of Parliament.

It's an extraordinary precedent.

One which not only denies Londoners their

say, but which also denies Parliament its rightful role in the process by which Government policies are implemented.

All along, the Government has made it clear it isn't going to let Londoners decide how London's run. Now it seems it isn't going to let Parliament decide either. **SAY NO TO NO SAY.**

Patrick Jenkin as dictator. The GLC made great play with two controversial provisions in the Local Government Bill: the power given to the DoE to control joint boards for three years, and Clause 93, which allowed Mr Jenkin to make 'consequential' or 'supplementary' changes after the abolition measure had become law.

against the government on a censure motion and had criticized the government's economic policies, saying that if the prime minister continued with them she would destroy the Tory Party. So, in an almost unprecedented action, Lord Alport, at the age of 71, had the whip withdrawn after more than 50 years for daring to criticize.

The government was clearly in troubled Tory waters as detailed consideration of the Abolition Bill began. It moved off to the Commons upstairs committee room corridor to be considered by an exceptionally large standing committee of 47 members. There were 15 Labour, three Alliance and 29 Tories, most of whom had been picked on the basis that they would be unlikely to rebel at any point during the Bill's sitting. Patrick Jenkin was not among them; demoralized and debilitated, he had opted to leave the business of defending the proposals word by word for hours on end to his more robust Local Government Minister, Kenneth Baker, who had already decided that from here on the subject could be dealt with only as pure politics.

The Lords

As with previous Bills, the government was left deciding whether to amend it when the committee stage was reported back to the Commons, in the hope of soothing the Lords, or whether to leave the Lords to do their worst, as they had with the abolition Paving Bill.

Mrs Thatcher remained keen not to 'give' on London unless the Lords delayed the Bill for so long that it was still there in July 1985, jeopardizing Royal Assent by the crucial target month of November. But senior Tories were already conceding that the government would now be lucky to get away without a London authority of some sort (adding that it was therefore a tragic pity to have missed an opportunity to do something proper and considered in the first place).

The Lords are likely to concentrate on two aspects of the Bill. The first is London, where the Cormack Amendment which narrowly failed in the Commons seems likely to be resurrected and, on the basis of the Commons vote, seems most likely to attract wide cross-party support. The second is the issue of reserve powers. It would be surprising for the Lords, given their usual approach to legislation, to allow the Bill to proceed in a way which gives the Secretary of State so much scope to take control of whatever he likes when he likes without further recourse to parliament.

After the GLC

So it still seems almost certain that sooner or later London will have some form of city-wide elected council, either on smaller areas such as the inner London boroughs covered by the Inner London Education Authority or on a Greater London area with fewer powers than the present GLC.

However, if it is 'later' and the abolition proceeds with no London authority of any sort to replace the GLC, the capital will surely experience a chaotic period of administration from April 1986.

Firstly, there are no signs whatever that the local government unions are prepared to allow their members to cooperate in the dismantling of the GLC. The government has so far been unable to acquire any detailed information about the GLC – it does not even know the size of its property portfolio, the profile of its property freeholds and leaseholds, or which properties in London the GLC owns. The potential for disruptive union action and non-cooperation is enormous, particularly because of the use of computer software files with passwords and codes.

Secondly, there is a sense of political solidarity with the GLC campaign to save itself among a number of the Labour-controlled London boroughs. They therefore also show no sign of being prepared to cooperate with the government.

Thirdly, the setting up of a plethora of joint boards and joint committees, especially in a hostile environment, is going to be complicated, protracted and expensive. Each will need a secretariat, accommodation, staff and a *modus operandi*, all of which take time and money.

The principal paymaster, of course, is the taxpayer – mainly the local taxpayer which, in this case, means the London rate-payer. Whatever the long-term savings from any abolition –

and the best indications from various independent management consultants are that they will either be non-existent or negligible – the short-term transition costs will be high. The government will be unable to avoid paying some, but the ratepayer will be saddled with the rest. And a London rate bill is going to look pretty daunting after 1986: a rate to the London borough, a rate to the Metropolitan Police, a rate to the Inner London Education Authority, a rate to London Regional Transport, a rate to the Fire Board ...

As the greater number of rating components to the London rate bill plus the expense of getting it all into gear is likely to mean Londoners paying more rather than less, the government is certainly going to need some of its reserve powers and controls in the early years.

This leads us to the next stage of the scenario for the future. The government has already taken control of the spending of the greater proportion of London boroughs through the Rates Act, which it is using to limit their expenditure and rate rises. This also applies to the ILEA. The Abolition Bill allows the government to intervene to control the budgets and manpower of all the new authorities for three years.

This means that virtually the whole of London's local government – and certainly its major services of fire, police and transport – will, one way or another, be under direct or potential central control. The complexity of administering these arrangements from Whitehall will lead to the creation of a 'London' section at the Environment Department and a minister will have to take first responsibility for the capital's arrangements – a minister for London. A minister or, more centralist still, a Ministry for London will represent the ultimate swing away from democratic and accountable localism.

Thereafter, the pendulum will surely start to swing back. Experience shows that while people often do not like local government they dislike central controls even more, and demands for local representation arise quickly.

When that will happen and under what political party in control of parliament is an open question. The Labour Party in power, for example, might enjoy the degree of centralism initiated by the Conservatives. It is inconceivable, on the other hand, that the Tories in opposition could or would have acquiesced to the central powers which they are now giving themselves.

So whatever happens the debate will go on and the pressure for a London-wide elected body is likely to be irresistible, either almost instantly, when their Lordships consider the Abolition Bill, or later when its effects are found to be not what anybody, the present government included, had in mind.

After all, the administration of London has held a prominent place in political debate for more than a century, and there is no sign that anyone is yet tiring of the argument. As Johnson said to Boswell: 'When a man is tired of London he is tired of life.'

Appendix:

Landmarks in the History of London Local Government

1829	Metropolitan Police established.
1835	Municipal Corporations Act sets up elected councils in English towns. London is excluded.
1848–9	Cholera epidemics lead to new concern about lack of proper sewers.
1855	Metropolitan Board of Works set up. Boundaries set become basis of later London County Council (LCC).
1884	Attempt to establish single elected London council by Liberal government fails.
1889	London County Council established. City of London excluded from provisions of the Act.
1899	Metropolitan Boroughs set up to reduce power of 'megalomaniac' LCC.
1907–34	Period of 'Municipal Reformer' majority in LCC.
1922	County Hall opened on South Bank.
1923	Ullswater Commission turns down plan for 'Greater London Council'.
1934–40	Herbert Morrison leads Labour LCC. Waterloo Bridge controversy.
1939	Conservative Central Office concludes LCC needs reform because of prospect of unending Labour rule.

1957	Herbert Commission established to examine 'the working of local government in the *Greater London* area'.
1960	Herbert recommends a 'council for Greater London'.
1963	London Government Act sets up GLC and 32 London boroughs. City of London remains separate unit.
1964	First GLC elections – Labour wins majority of 28.
1965	Milner Holland Report on London Housing – endorses redistribution of population, acquisition in suburbs and a strong central housing authority.
1965–7	Labour GLC attempts to develop housing strategy – rebuffed by boroughs.
1967	Conservatives capture GLC with majority of 64.
1967–70	Horace Cutler winds down GLC housing programme.
1969	First draft of Greater London Development Plan (GLDP). London Transport is transferred to GLC control.
1970	Tories hold on to GLC control in elections. Majority reduced to 30.
1970–2	GLC housing policy again blocked by boroughs.
1972	Layfield Inquiry into GLDP reports. Highly critical of GLC planners.

1973	Labour regains control of GLC with majority of 24. 'Motorway Box' plan thrown out.
1975	Collapse of Labour's 'Housing Strategy Plan'.
1976	GLDP finally approved by GLC, heavily amended.
1977	Conservative victory in GLC elections – majority of 36. Horace Cutler becomes leader.
1978	Marshall Report on London government. Evidence by Patrick Jenkin and Kenneth Baker in favour of GLC.
March 1979	Ken Livingstone calls for abolition of the GLC.
May 1979	Mrs Thatcher becomes Prime Minister.
1980	GLC transfers majority of its dwellings to the London boroughs.
February 1980	First issue of the left-wing monthly, *London Labour Briefing*, launched by Ken Livingstone.
April 1980	Reg Goodwin, Labour opposition leader of the GLC, resigns.
May 1980	Andrew McIntosh elected as new Labour Group leader, beating Ken Livingstone by one vote.
7 May 1981	Labour wins the GLC elections with a majority of eight.
8 May 1981	Ken Livingstone defeats Andrew McIntosh by 10 votes to become GLC leader.

June to July 1981	Press hostility against Livingstone over his views on Ireland, gays and royalty reaches a peak.
October 1981	'Fares Fair' introduced, cutting London Transport fares by 32 per cent at the cost of a supplementary rate of 11.9p in the $\pounds$.
14 October 1981	The *Sun* describes Ken Livingstone as 'the most odious man in Britain' after he was alleged, but disputed, to have refused to brand IRA bombers as criminals.
17 December 1981	The House of Lords rules the GLC's cheap fares policy unlawful.

Countdown to abolition

May 1983	Mrs Thatcher decides to include abolition in her election manifesto.
9 June 1983	The Conservatives win the general election. Patrick Jenkin is appointed as Secretary of State for the Environment.
20 September 1983	The Cabinet subcommittee on abolition (Misc 95) recommends that the GLC elections due in May 1985 should be cancelled, and that for the remaining eleven months until abolition in April 1986, the GLC should be 'run' by an interim body of councillors appointed by the boroughs. Even though this means switching political control from Labour to Conservative, Mrs Thatcher subsequently agrees, though with reluctance.
7 October 1983	The White Paper, *Streamlining the Cities*, is published.
March 1984	The first anti-abolition posters appear in

the GLC's 'Say No to No Say' campaign. A *MORI/Standard* poll shows 61 per cent of Londoners opposed to abolition and only 22 per cent for.

30 March 1984   The 'Paving Bill' (The Local Government, Interim Provisions Bill) is published providing for the cancellation of the GLC elections and the substitution of borough councillors.

11 April 1984   During the second reading of the Paving Bill in the House of Commons, there is strong criticism from leading Conservatives, including Edward Heath, Ian Gilmour and Francis Pym; 19 Tories vote against the government.

11 June 1984   During the second reading of the Paving Bill in the House of Lords, a wrecking amendment tabled by Labour and Alliance peers, describing the Bill as a 'dangerous precedent', is defeated by only 20 votes.

28 June 1984   The government is heavily defeated by 48 votes on an all-party amendment designed to wreck the Bill.

July 1984   Amid much embarrassment, the government reluctantly agrees to amend the Bill to extend the life of the existing GLC for one year, thereby leaving Ken Livingstone in power for this additional period.

26 July 1984   The Paving Bill becomes law.

2 August 1984   Ken Livingstone and three colleagues resign their GLC seats in order to fight by-elections on the principle of abolition. These elections are boycotted by the Tories.

10 September 1984   Mrs Thatcher replaces Lord Bellwin with
Kenneth Baker as Local Government
Minister.

20 September 1984   Labour wins all four by-elections with
large majorities but on very low turnouts.

22 November 1984   The Local Government Bill providing for
abolition is finally published. It has
98 clauses and 17 schedules.

3/4 December 1984   During the debate on the second reading
of the Bill, Patrick Jenkin is 'savaged'
by his own backbenchers.

14 December 1984   At 12.37 a.m. at the end of a two-day
debate on the committee stage held on
the floor of the House, the government's
majority slumps to 23 on an amendment
moved by a Tory, Patrick Cormack, that
the GLC should be replaced by a directly
elected authority with functions
determined following an inquiry by a
Commons select committee.

Select Bibliography

Ali, T., *Who's Afraid of Margaret Thatcher?* (London, Verso, 1984)

Burgess, T. and Travers, T., *Local Government in Greater London and the Metropolitan Counties: a Response to the Government's Proposals* (North East London Polytechnic, 1984)

Carvel, J., *Citizen Ken* (London, Chatto & Windus, The Hogarth Press, 1984)

Coopers & Lybrand Associates, *Streamlining the Cities: Analysis of the Costs* (London, Coopers & Lybrand, 1984)

Department of the Environment, *Streamlining the Cities: Government Proposals for Reorganising Local Government in Greater London and the Metropolitan Counties* (The White Paper) (London, HMSO, Cmnd. 9063, 1983)

DoE, *Abolition of the Greater London Council and the Metropolitan Counties* (The Yellow Paper) (London, DoE, 1984)

Flynn, N. and Leach, S., *Joint Boards and Joint Committees: an Evaluation* (Birmingham, Institute of Local Government Studies, 1984)

Foster, C. D., Jackman, R., Perlman, M., *Local Government Finance in a Unitary State* (London, George Allen & Unwin, 1980)

Hall, P., *London 2000*, 2nd edn (London, Faber, 1969)

House of Commons, *Fifth Report from the Transport Committee, 1981–2. Transport in London* (London, HMSO, 1982)

Jones, G. W. and Donoughue, B., *Herbert Morrison, Portrait of a Politician* (London, Weidenfeld & Nicolson, 1973)

London Journal, *London After the GLC* (Vol. 10, No. 1, Summer 1984)

Marshall, Sir Frank, *The Marshall Inquiry on Greater London* (London, GLC, 1978)

Norton, A., *The Government and Administration of Metropolitan Authorities in Western Democracies* (Birmingham, Institute of Local Government Studies, 1983)

Richards, P. G., *The Reformed Local Government System* (London, George Allen & Unwin, 1976)

Stewart, J., *Local Government: The Conditions of Local Choice* (London, George Allen & Unwin, 1983)

University College, London and London School of Economics and Political Science, *Governing London* (Conference Proceedings) (London, UCL and LSE, 1984)

Young, K. and Kramer, J., *Strategy and Conflict in Metropolitan Housing* (London, Arnold, 1978)

Young, K. and Garside, P., *Metropolitan London* (London, Arnold, 1982)

Index